PUB STROLLS IN

ESSEX

Ann and
Norman Skinner

COUNTRYSIDE BOOKS
NEWBURY BERKSHIRE

First published 2000
© Ann and Norman Skinner 2000

COUNTRYSIDE BOOKS
3 Catherine Road
Newbury, Berkshire

To view our complete range of books,
please visit us at
www.countrysidebooks.co.uk

ISBN 1 85306 619 2

Designed by Graham Whiteman
Photographs by Ann Skinner
Maps by Gelder design & mapping

Produced through MRM Associates Ltd., Reading
Printed by WBC Book Manufacturers Ltd., Bridgend

Contents

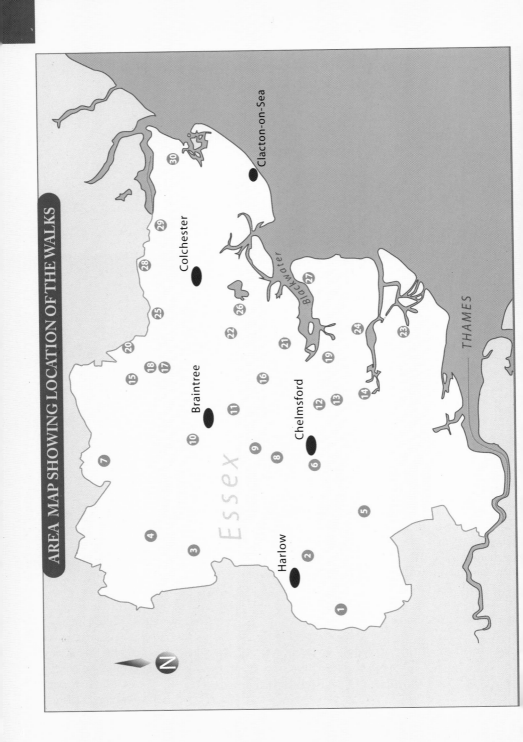

AREA MAP SHOWING LOCATION OF THE WALKS

PUBLISHER'S NOTE

We hope that you obtain considerable enjoyment from this book; great care has been taken in its preparation. However, changes of landlord and actual closures are sadly not uncommon. Likewise, although at the time of publication all routes followed public rights of ways or permitted paths, diversion orders can be made and permissions withdrawn.

We cannot, of course, be held responsible for such diversion orders and any inaccuracies in the text which result from these or any other changes to the routes nor any damage which might result from walkers trespassing on private property. We are anxious though that all details covering the walks and the pubs are kept up to date and would therefore welcome information from readers which would be relevant to future editions.

The sketch maps accompanying each walk are not always to scale and are intended to guide you to the starting point and give a simple but accurate idea of the route to be taken. For those who like the benefit of detailed maps, we recommend that you arm yourself with the relevant Ordnance Survey sheet in either the Pathfinder or Explorer series.

Welcome, dear reader, to *Pub Strolls in Essex*. We have set up a series of 30 of what we hope you will find are relatively easy walks, varying in length from $1^1/_2$ to 4 miles. We have tried to go to fresh places, and all the walks are completely new. We hope you will enjoy the same sense of excitement that we have had when you take to the open road!

We have tried to visit as many corners of our beautiful county as possible. With a county as large as Essex I am sure, like us, you will be expecting varieties in terrain and you will not be disappointed in this respect. We found some of the hills took our breath away, but then the views from others were also quite breath taking. You will walk in river valleys, through woods, and over open fields as well as along country lanes and roads. And if you want to make it a full day out, we also give suggestions for places of interest nearby that you may like to visit.

So what of the pubs we can hear the beer buffs muttering. Essex is not a county where every other pub has a picturesque thatched roof. But we have been rather surprised to find so many ordinary looking pubs were actually over 300 years old. Many pubs have fine wooden beams. The range of old chimneys often with log fires in the cooler weather is again a surprise. So many of the landlords we have spoken with have an interest in and knowledge of the building in which they currently live and work. We have found an interesting range of beers, lagers, ciders and wine served in a variety of bars from busy out-of-town eating houses to simple country pubs. We have also found a wonderful range of tempting food on offer.

We have designed the walks with the idea that you will have your meal first so that you can then ask the landlord in person about parking while you do the walk. But you may be an early bird and wish to walk first then eat. This is not a problem but in this case please ring the day before and ask permission to park so the landlord is not left wondering, 'Who does that strange car belong to?'

What should you take with you on the stroll? Even though you will be undertaking a short outing we do recommend the relevant Ordnance Survey map. All the sketch maps are drawn with north at the top, but are not to any given scale. We have added numbers so you can more easily relate the text on the stroll description to the map. If you like a simple drink and a rest break part way through the stroll then a small bottle of fizzy water or a flask of tea or coffee may be your choice to accompany you while you stop and admire the view.

Depending on the weather and the season of the year, footwear is one of the most important elements. Should it be summer and warm and sunny, trainers or sandals are appropriate. On colder days stout walking shoes or boots can be better especially if showers are predicted. For wet walks especially if muddy there is nothing like the ubiquitous wellies. Whilst on the subject of footwear, it is not so popular to enter the pub with dirty shoes so please carry a change in the car. The good name of the walking fraternity may depend on you!

All that remains is to wish you many happy days out, happy strolling and whenever you get to the pub, cheers!

Ann and Norman Skinner

Upshire
The Horseshoes

| MAP: OS EXPLORER 174 (GR 414011) | **WALK 1** | DISTANCE: 1¾ MILES |

DIRECTIONS TO START: FROM EPPING TAKE THE B1393 SOUTH-WEST. ABOUT 1 MILE AFTER CROSSING THE M25 TURN RIGHT ON UPSHIRE ROAD. AFTER 1½ MILES YOU COME TO UPSHIRE CHURCH. **PARKING:** PARK IN THE HORSESHOES CAR PARK. PLEASE ASK THE LANDLORD IF YOU CAN LEAVE YOUR CAR WHILST YOU COMPLETE THE WALK.

Upshire, set in one of the hillier parts of west Essex, is a gem of a village dominated by St Thomas's parish church and the delightful row of ancient Essex weatherboarded cottages. During this short stroll you will enjoy some wonderful views, from high above the motorway towards Enfield. Now follows a hedged lane again with good views, this time over Upshirebury Green. Another green lane and a path lead to the pretty Lodge at Warlies and a sedate path through the estate passes to the rear of Warlies itself. On the short climb back to your car and the pub, the views are over Temple Hill and towards Epping.

The Horseshoes

This brick and timbered building, where you can rest in comfort with your food and drink, is set high amongst the hills of Upshire. Inside you come straight to the bar. You will find the usual range of pub grub including mini French bread rolls, ploughman's and jacket potatoes, along with a range of salads. Fillings like prawns, ham, beef and cheese are available. The main menu gives a choice of cooked food including scampi, cod and chips, lasagne, and shepherds pie. You should find McMullen Original AK, and Cream Ale and Pilsner; also Strongbow cider on hand pump and Woodpecker in bottles. Telephone: 01992 712745.

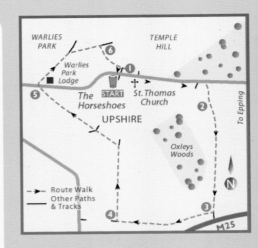

The Walk

① Turn left out of the car park and walk uphill past the village hall and St Thomas's church. As the road bends left you make

The Lodge at Warlies.

Warlies Park.

your way right up the gravel drive to the double bridleway sign.

② Go straight on, passing the Woodredon and Warlies Park Estate sign. A gate marks the entrance to the gravel drive that goes to the very edge of the M25.

③ Just before the drive becomes a bridge over the motorway, turn right and walk high above the motorway on a fenced bridleway. After about 250 yards the path swings right and you will find yourself going downhill.

④ At the path junction turn right on bridleway path number 96. It is marked 'Copthall Green ½ mile'. As the path begins to flatten, turn left on a wide grassy track. There were no arrows or signs to assist you with this turn when we walked it but after about 100 yards you will walk past a stile on your right, which you ignore. The track becomes a gravel road as you walk past four rural cottage homes. When the gravel road turns right keep straight ahead to cross a meadow and exit the path onto a road opposite the Warlies Park Lodge at the public bridleway sign.

⑤ Cross the road with care and walk to the left of the Lodge past a bridleway sign on an estate road. At the gates take the stile just to the right of them and walk between the wooden fence and the drive. When you come to a gate on your right take this into the meadow.

⑥ Now follows an uphill climb to the gate you can just see at the top. Go through the gate and the car park is just a further 25 paces up ahead of you.

Foster Street
The Horns and Horseshoes

MAP: OS EXPLORER 174 (GR 486087) | **WALK 2** | **DISTANCE:** 2¼ MILES

DIRECTIONS TO START: FROM THE M11/A414 ROUNDABOUT JUNCTION TAKE THE HASTINGWOOD ROAD (NORTH-EAST). JUST PAST HASTINGWOOD TURN LEFT AT SHONK'S FARM AND AFTER A FURTHER ¾ MILE COME TO A T JUNCTION. TURN RIGHT AND ALMOST STRAIGHTAWAY RIGHT AGAIN. THE PUB IS ON YOUR LEFT. **PARKING:** PARK IN THE PUB CAR PARK AT THE REAR. MAKE SURE YOU ASK PERMISSION TO LEAVE YOUR CAR BEFORE YOU START THE WALK.

This walk, separated from East Harlow and Potter Street by the M11, is surprisingly quiet and rural. It is in the unusual position of being sandwiched between two well known long distance routes. The Forest Way passes about 50 yards north of the pub and the Stort Valley Way passes through Hastingwood village about ¼ mile from Shonk's Farm, so you are in a popular walking area. Your stroll starts along two field-edge green lanes. Then follows a wide green bridleway that brings you back to Shonk's Farm, a country road and a meadow where horses often graze, to bring you to within yards of the byway and your return route to the pub.

The Horns and Horseshoes

The pub has a rather low ceiling and your first impression is of wooden beams, gleaming brass and a number of tables placed in discreet alcoves, while the bar is sited to one side. I don't think I have ever seen so many brasses assembled in one place! Courage Best and Directors bitters are on offer along with the full range of cider, lager, wine etc. The menu choices go through the usual selection of jacket potatoes, sandwiches, ploughman's and baguettes. You may be tempted by a salad, plaice, cod, scampi or chilli. Sausage and mash, ham, egg and chips, quarterpounders, chicken in a bun and children's meals are also available at reasonable prices. Telephone: 01279 422667.

The Walk

① Turn left out of the pub and walk south-east. As the lane turns left so do you. You are on a byway which will take you for just over ½ mile to the road at Green Lane.

② Turn right to pick up another byway (this was reached over some rubble at the time I walked it out). It starts as a hedged green lane. As it opens out you will spot a large field on your right.

③ As the field ends turn right and walk along the wide green lane with white marker posts. Pass on your left a bridge installed by the West Essex Group of the Ramblers. You will soon come to the road and bridleway sign.

④ Turn right and right again into Mill Street. Now follows a ½ mile road walk.

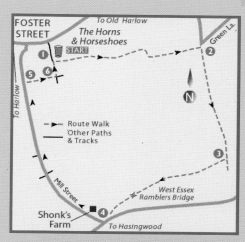

Pass by the first footpath sign on your right.

⑤ You are looking for the second footpath sign. Walk down the drive to the right of a house. As it ends go over a fence into the field and continue in the same direction with the hedge on your left. In the far left-hand corner of the field you will find a stile, go over this.

⑥ Turn left and go about ⅛ mile (this short part of the route can sometimes be muddy) back to the byway you used on the way out, and the car park.

PLACES OF INTEREST NEARBY

The **Gibberd Collection** in the Town Hall, The High, Harlow is a collection of British water-colours. Telephone 01279 446763 for opening hours.

The **Mark Hall Cycle Museum and Gardens**, Muskham Road, Harlow has a collection of cycles from 1818 set in a converted stable block with three period walled gardens to view. Telephone 01279 439680 for more information.

On the route.

Manuden
The Yew Tree Inn

DIRECTIONS TO START: MANUDEN IS CLOSE TO THE WESTERN BORDER OF ESSEX, NORTH-WEST OF STANSTED MOUNTFITCHET. THE YEW TREE INN IS CLOSE BY THE CHURCH WHICH DOMINATES THE VILLAGE. **PARKING:** PARK AT THE PUB, PREFERABLY ROUND THE BACK OF THE LARGE CAR PARK. PLEASE LET THE LANDLORD KNOW THAT YOU HAVE LEFT YOUR CAR TO GO ON THE STROLL.

Manuden is a picturesque and ancient village in an attractive setting in the valley of the River Stort. There is much to enjoy here – the white timbered cottages, the overhanging eaves, and the treasures of carved wood in the church. It was at Manuden on 29th May, until about 100 years ago, that 'Bumping Day' was celebrated, when the young men of the village unceremoniously 'bumped' everyone they met. This is a lovely walk of green paths and woodland, with wide views all around, taking you out to the delightfully named Chatter End and returning by stream and pond.

The Yew Tree Inn

The Yew Tree Inn is a fine example of a village pub. Beers to choose from are Greene King IPA and Abbott, with Marston's Pedigree as an alternative. The bar is central in a fairly large room with some window seats that form alcoves where you can sit in comfort in small family groups. The walls of the bar carry various pictures of the village. A restaurant has been built on in recent times for the evening, or perhaps a large party. The landlord is welcoming and friendly to walkers and is able to offer bed and breakfast accommodation at the pub. The food is announced by a lunch time menu and an evening menu. Daily specials, of which there may be eight or ten, are on a large blackboard. We chose lamb in red wine sauce but fish and vegetarian choices are also available. Telephone: 01279 812888.

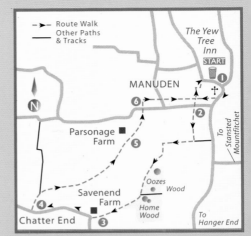

The Walk

① From the pub walk back the way you drove in on for a few yards and spot a footpath signpost on the right leading into the churchyard. Pass to the left of the church, between it and a row of splendid old houses. At the end of the churchyard go out onto a pathway and immediately turn left. Soon you cross a road and climb steps to walk a field-edge path.

② Pass allotments and when you come to a post with yellow arrows turn right onto a farm track, climbing to the end of the field. Turn left along the field edge and very soon take a right diagonal path aiming for the right-hand corner of the woods ahead. Now you follow the edge of the wood going south. Ignore a left turn at a corner but bear right, now going west. At the corner turn left into a shaded path through trees to cross a bridge and by a gate into a large pasture field. Walk with the hedge on your right till you reach a large oak tree. Now bear left to a five-barred gate in the corner at Savenend Farm.

③ From the gate walk out to a road and turn right for 200 yards up to the quaintly named Chatter End.

④ Turn right past the last house and follow the path downhill. Cross a bridge at the field corner and turn right with a fence on your right to a gap in the hedge leading into the next field. Now turn right along a

PLACES OF INTEREST NEARBY

At **Stansted Mountfitchet** you can experience what life was like in a Norman castle and village, marvel at the siege weapons – including two giant catapults – and mingle with the many animals that roam freely through the ancient site. Telephone: 01279 813237. Then visit the House on the Hill Toy Museum adjacent to the Castle.

Old cottages on the edge of the churchyard.

farm track with wide views all around. The track leads downhill and crosses a stream before going uphill to reach Parsonage Farm. The hedge has been on your left. Follow the track through the hedge and immediately turn right with the hedge on your right.

⑤ When this hedge ends, bear left along a rough grassy path midway between a pond on your left and a pond on your right. This leads through a gap in the hedge ahead and you walk by the side of another pond. At the end of the pond turn left across a small field to a road with footpath signs in all directions. Cross the road into a hedged green lane.

⑥ After a few yards turn right into a large field. The path which runs parallel to a hedge on your right is 10 yards inside the field and is usually reinstated by the farmer. Walk towards a thatched cottage. Now cross into the next field and continue on a good grass path down to a broad earth path. Turn left and follow this path round the churchyard out to the road. The Yew Tree Inn is 50 yards to the right.

Widdington
The Fleur de Lys

MAP: OS EXPLORER 195 (GR 538317)	WALK 4	DISTANCE: 3½ MILES

DIRECTIONS TO START: FROM STANSTED MOUNTFITCHET DRIVE NORTH ON THE B1383.
BEFORE NEWPORT FOLLOW THE ROAD TO THE RIGHT SIGNPOSTED WIDDINGTON.
PARKING: AT THE PUB. PLEASE ASK PERMISSION BEFORE STARTING OUT
ON THE WALK.

Widdington is a small village with an attractive green near the source of the River Cam, with a long history. Priors Hall nearby has stone walls behind the plaster which are believed to be almost as old as Magna Carta. Just outside the village is Mole Hall, a moated house lying a mile to the south-east along a narrow lane, where the owners have established a fascinating wildlife park. At Mole Hall you may stumble over a deer, or come face to face with a pelican! This lovely stroll takes you past the park, before joining the River Cam for a short time and returning by a woodland path.

The Fleur de Lys

In the church at Widdington is a 14th century stained glass window depicting the shields of France and of England. Perhaps the French connection accounts for the pub being named the Fleurs de Lys. This is an excellent local. They have a fine selection of beers – Adnams, Bass, Batemans XB and Burton Ale, with guest beers. The choice of food is excellent, and the jacket potatoes and baguettes have a wide selection of fillings if it is a snack you seek. The main meals include a choice of specials such as huge portions of fish and chips. The chalk-board is changed daily and we were tempted by the chicken breasts in a rich cream prawn and mushroom sauce. Telephone: 01799 540659.

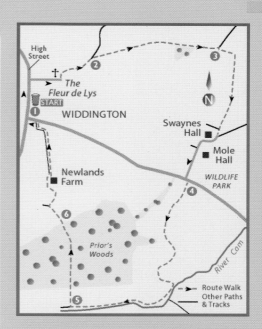

The Walk

① Leave the pub and turn right along the High Street. In a few yards turn right at the green and walk past the church. Immediately turn left at a concrete public footpath sign with a hedge on your right. Reaching a field, turn right along a good headland.

② The path bears left for 175 yards. At the field corner turn right along a field edge. At the next corner continue across the open field to the left of the wood ahead. Cross a ditch to the left and continue with the wood on your right to a facing hedge.

③ Cross the ditch on an earth bridge by the gap and turn right round the field corner. As you pass the hedge on the right, turn right through the ditch and walk uphill (south) towards buildings (Swaynes Hall). On reaching a public footpath sign turn right and join a farm road between farm buildings and the Hall. Follow the road past Mole Hall Wildlife Reserve, turn left with the animals still on your left and reach a road.

④ Cross by the Byway sign and enter a hedged path. Follow this as it wends its way southwards. After ¼ mile the path is joined by the River Cam and shortly turns right passing a bridge to continue west.

PLACES OF INTEREST NEARBY

Mole Hall Wildlife Park passed on the walk is well worth a visit. It is open daily 10.30 am to 6 pm (dusk in winter). Telephone: 01799 540400.

Priors Hall Barn at Widdington, admission free, is one of the finest aisled barns in south-east England. Open April to September. Telephone: 0179 522842.

A delightful cottage passed on the walk.

⑤ After 600 yards carefully look for a yellow arrow on the right and turn right across the field towards Priors Wood. If you come to a house you have missed the waymark and need to retrace 130 yards. Reach the wood by a gate and another yellow arrow. You should walk on through the wood on a broad path.

⑥ At the end of the wood turn left and soon turn right at an arrow and over the stile. At the path junction turn right. Ignore the arrow to the left and turn right at the tennis court over two stiles. Continue with a fence on the left. Cross another stile and exit through a white gate to a public footpath sign. At Newlands Farm follow the sign left round the garden past a large pond to a stile in the far north-east corner. Ignore the stile and turn left through the gate to walk with a hedge on your right. Cross a stile with an arrow and walk on, turning left and right to Cornells Lane. Turn left for a few yards to the road and right to the Fleur de Lys.

Doddinghurst
The Moat

MAP: OS EXPLORER 175 (GR 590990)   **WALK 5**   **DISTANCE:** 2½ MILES

DIRECTIONS TO START: DODDINGHURST, WITH THE MOAT IN THE VILLAGE CENTRE, IS SITUATED PARTWAY BETWEEN MOUNTNESSING ON THE A12 AND KELVEDON HATCH ON THE A128. **PARKING:** YOU MAY LEAVE YOUR CAR IN THE MOAT CAR PARK.

The village of Doddinghurst dates back to at least the 13th century, though it has changed much over recent years. This pleasant stroll takes you out of the village to enjoy lovely views over the countryside towards Stondon Massey. On your return route, the large loop came about because a garden of one of the houses was extended over the footpath, and this enjoyable woodland walk is the result of hard negotiations over many years. The final series of twittens (alleys) return you to the beautiful 13th century village church. It is said to have one of the best wooden porches in Essex and the Tudor house that was once the home of the priest is still used by churchgoers for coffee mornings and the like.

The Moat

The village pub has been under new management since 1998. The building is of red brick, with high ceilings, beams, picture and dado rails, set off by a fine collection of brasses and plates. The restaurant doubles as a children's room or meeting room and is available for an à la carte menu. The main bar snacks at lunch time are sandwiches, baguettes, ploughman's and jacket potatoes. There is a wide range of fillings to choose from. You may be tempted by the set menu of two or three courses at a very competitive price. The range of drinks include keg Caffreys, Guinness, Stella Artois and Boddingtons. On hand pump are Woodcocks IPA and Abbott. Strongbow is the cider available. Telephone: 01277 821650.

The Walk

① From the Moat turn right and walk past the parade of shops. Turn right into All Saints Close. Take the twitten between numbers 12 and 13. On reaching The Gardens cross over to number 36 and turn right to follow this road round the bend. On reaching number 12, turn right and walk out to the main road.

② At the T junction cross half-left to a footpath sign to the right of Lympstone. Walk uphill with the fence on your left. You cross a two-sleeper bridge and walk straight on uphill. Ignore a series of paths to your left round the field, and exit the field in the top right-hand corner. Walk along the right-hand side of the field to a stile and Hook End Road. A footpath sign confirms you have come out in the right place.

③ Turn left. Now follows an interesting walk past houses that have been added to in a variety of ways, and some little resemble their more humble past. Once Hook End Road becomes Blackmore Road-Deal Tree corner, cross to the pedestrian footway. Turn right and follow this path to the 16th century Soap House.

④ As you exit the footpath turn immediately left into the RUPP (a Road Used as a Public Path). Walk south-west. There are excellent views right towards Stondon Massey. It takes you about ½ mile between fields on a normally firm and dry route to reach the road.

⑤ At School Road turn left; this road can sometimes be very busy so take care. At the next T junction, Blackmore Road, cross to the footpath sign at the end of the drive to Doddinghurst Place. When you reach the notice 'Churchwood Fisheries' the arrow informs you the path is straight on to the right of a small brick wall.

⑥ As you enter the meadow head half-left to the stile and waymark. You now enter a

The village church at Doddinghurst.

PLACES OF INTEREST NEARBY

Brentwood Centre, Doddinghurst Road, Brentwood has sporting and fitness facilities including a swimming pool. It is also a top entertainment venue for shows, concerts, and bands. Telephone: 01277 262616.

The windmill at **Mountnessing** does have open days. Telephone: Brentwood Tourist Information Centre on 01277 200300 for details.

recently planted wooded area. You are heading half-left to the footpath sign under the large oak. Your route is to the left of the pond and another yellow arrow under another large oak tree. The first ten steps or so as you leave the pond can at times get very overgrown. A cross-field path takes you out to the road in Church Lane, Doddinghurst. Climb over the stile and go left for 10 yards to another footpath sign.

(7) Cross the stile. This path passes the back of several gardens before turning left along the edge of the wood. A series of footpath signs should now guide your route, but some arrows were missing the day we walked it. When you come to the pond turn right, north. Cross the wooden bridge and make your way to the northern edge of the wood. Turn right. At the next arrow turn right again on a well walked downhill path and cross the wooden walkway.

(8) Keep the wire fence on your right as you make your way over a further wooden bridge to an arrow. Here turn left and go down three steps and through a kissing gate. Enter the twitten and go out to the road. Immediately turn right and right again to enter a further twitten next door to number 65. This brings you into the back of the churchyard. Walk to the right of the church. You will see the old priest house on your right. Take the path in front of the church porch and exit the churchyard by a little wooden gate. Turn left and return to the pub on the route you know.

Writtle
The Inn on the Green

MAP: OS EXPLORER 183 (GR 676063)   **WALK 6**   **DISTANCE:** 3¼ MILES

DIRECTIONS TO START: FROM CHELMSFORD TAKE THE A1060 WEST OUT OF TOWN. AT THE SIGN FOR WRITTLE YOU GO SOUTH PAST THE COLLEGE. AT THE GARAGE TURN LEFT INTO THE GREEN. THE INN ON THE GREEN IS THE FIRST PUB ON YOUR RIGHT JUST BEFORE THE GREEN. **PARKING:** PLEASE ASK THE LANDLORD'S PERMISSION BEFORE LEAVING YOUR CAR TO DO THE WALK.

This fascinating walk from Writtle starts with a stroll along the edge of the lovely village green towards Aubyns, a beautiful timbered house. From All Saints church follows a short walk through the centre of the village to St John's Green with its collection of superb old and newer houses. At Melba Court you may wish to take a few steps to the right to read the notice about Marconi and historic radio broadcasts. Lawford Lane, the old main road into Chelmsford, is now a hedged track and your route takes you north-east to the edge of the River Can, before returning through the grounds of Writtle Agricultural College.

The Inn on the Green

This traditional old pub has one large oak-beamed bar with a raised dais at one end. A series of alcoves, a central oval bar and many dining chairs give you the feeling you are to be fed well here. They even have a restaurant to house the overspill at busy meal times. The large garden is to the left of the pub behind the car park. There are several exciting chalk menu boards to choose from. The selection of sandwich and jacket potato fillings includes everything I have ever thought of and then some more. The vegetarian choice that caught my eye was a Broccoli and Cream Cheese Bake. There is a range of starters including soup, peppered mackerel, and mushrooms with a garlic dip. The main courses included two curries, chilli, steak and kidney, and lasagne. My Sizzling Chicken Curry with rice was very good. For those with a sweet tooth the hot puddings include treacle sponge and spotted dick. Nethergate IPA, Regular Cottage Brewery and Mighty Oak are the usual beers but they are joined by guest beers on a regular basis. Thatchers cider by gravity will appeal to others while Henry Molyneux's choice of wines is available in red and white. Telephone 01245 420266 for more details.

The Walk

① Leave the Inn by walking right along a tree-lined road to the right of the green. When the road splits take the left fork towards Aubyns and Church Lane. Keep straight on through the wooden gates into the churchyard. The church is well worth a visit if you can spare the time.

② Exit the churchyard along a yew-lined path to a five-bar gate. Walk straight on with the red brick wall on your right. At the road ahead turn left. Cross the main road with care and enter St John's Green. A yellow arrow confirms your route. At the end of the green turn right, again the arrow confirms the route. You are now in Lawford Lane.

③ Just round the bend you will see the board about Marconi. This contains a little information about the history of the 'hut'. Retrace your steps to rejoin Lawford Lane and pass to the left of a six-bar metal gate. It is signed as a bridleway.

④ After nearly a mile you come to the River Can bridge. Do not cross this but go to your left through a wooden walkway. It is a shame no yellow arrow is here to confirm your route. Keep beside the river for about ¹/₂ mile.

⑤ When you reach the road by the footpath sign turn left and cross into Cow Watering Lane. Follow along this road for

The River Can.

about ⅔ mile till you come to a footpath sign on your left just before Reeds Cottage.

⑥ This footpath takes you to the right of a fence through the college land. Cross the gravel track when you reach it and go downhill and up the other side till you come to the brook.

⑦ Turn left and walk along the side of this 650 year old hedge. Continue along this hedge till you come to a footpath sign and a concrete bridge on your right over the brook. Turn half-left to a wooden stile under a tree. Cross the stile bridge and stile to enter a field. Walk with the barbed wire fence on your left. At the far left corner of the field cross a stile and turn left beside the yellow arrow.

⑧ Walk on a path to the edge of the allotments; it soon becomes a gravel track. Cross the road ahead and continue on the track to the main road. Cross to the small triangular green ahead and then walk ahead past the Wheatsheaf into The Green. The Inn on the Green is the first pub on your right.

Birdbrook
The Plough

MAP: OS PATHFINDER 1028 (GR 706411)   **WALK 7**   DISTANCE: 3¼ MILES

DIRECTIONS TO START: BIRDBROOK IS IN THE NORTH OF THE COUNTY, EAST OF STEEPLE BUMPSTEAD. **PARKING:** AT THE PLOUGH – PLEASE ASK FOR PERMISSION BEFORE SETTING OUT ON THE WALK.

Birdbrook is among the loveliest of Essex villages. The small village street has not been augmented by modern building, and to the great fortune of the residents retains to this day a variety of styles of architecture, some of it 500 years old. The outward route through peaceful countryside takes you across the infant River Colne. The adjoining Moyn's Park with its Elizabethan manor house is the setting for the final mile of a beautiful little walk, certainly a visit to remember.

The Plough

In the 18th century the village pub was known as the 'Swan'. Martha Blewitt was the then landlady and received notoriety for outliving eight husbands – but was buried by the ninth! A stone in the tower of the church records this remarkable fact. The Plough in the present time is a fine building in its own right, serving a changing selection of ales, cider and lagers. For seemingly such a neat little bar, the Plough is able to produce an excellent choice of food – sandwiches, baguettes, jacket potatoes and hot meals, i.e. steak pies, fish, spare ribs, lasagne and curries. Telephone: 01440 785336.

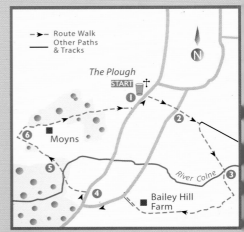

The Walk

① From the Plough turn right for a few yards and cross the road to join a footpath by a black public footpath sign. Walk into a hayfield and continue with the hedge on your left. The footpath should exit in the corner but it is more convenient to leave by a gap on the right.

② Cross the road and walk the farm track with a hedge still on your left. When the hedge ends walk half-right across the field downhill towards the brook to reach the bottom, by the left of a clump of trees taller than the rest of the crossing hedge. A path leads through the clump to a broad bridleway bridge which you cross. The tiny stream which you have crossed is in fact the River Colne barely 1½ miles after its birth in nearby Moyn's Park.

③ Follow the high hedge on your left uphill out of the river valley. At a path junction turn right to follow a good path, rising less steeply now and enabling you to look back over your right shoulder to Birdbrook village and church on the hilltop across the valley. The path continues through the steading of Bailey Hill Farm to a lane. Turn left. At the next T junction be not alarmed if your Ordnance Survey map shows a path which is not there! Turn right for 200 yards and left by a black public footpath sign – the path has been diverted to the field edge.

④ Walk down the farm track by a hedge on your left and cross the open field to find a bridge (again over the Colne) into Moyn's Park. We are now within the charms of the estate but have to negotiate five stiles to cross it.

⑤ After the first, turn left to cross a field to a stile bridge/stile combination. Bear right to the middle of the fence opposite

Moyn's Park.

and cross a stile. Turn half-right through some 'set aside' to the tree then turn right up a grass track in the centre of the field and leave by a gate at the top left corner. Turn right, keeping between the hedge and the electric fence round to a stile on your right. Follow the arrows through a hedge and continue till you reach a metal crossing track.

⑥ Turn right for a leisurely walk passing the magnificent 500 year old Elizabethan manor house. Maintain your line due east till you reach the road. Turn left, passing firstly the thatched village hall. On the short walk back to the Plough one would not wish one house changed. Every typical Essex style and material is represented here.

Little Waltham
The White Hart

MAP: OS EXPLORER 183 (GR 708131)   **WALK 8**   **DISTANCE:** 3¾ MILES

DIRECTIONS TO START: LITTLE WALTHAM LIES TO THE NORTH OF CHELMSFORD, EASILY REACHED OFF THE A130. **PARKING:** IN THE WHITE HART CAR PARK, AFTER ASKING THE LANDLORD'S PERMISSION, OR IF THE PUB IS CLOSED, PARK IN THE LAY BY OPPOSITE.

Leaving Little Waltham on your way to Sheepcotes Farm, you will enjoy views over the Chelmer Valley to Broomfield and walk a well marked field edge path. An old road-cum-green track heads for the much more modern golf course. The path has been diverted around the sides of the course and round the club house. Next follows an ancient path along the byway with good views over the Chelmer and the fishing lakes right down to Croxton Mill and weir. The final walk up through the old village of Little Waltham will for some become a much longer affair as you take time out in examining in more detail many of the delightful old properties that line your route back to the pub.

The White Hart

This is a pub of almost two halves – the public bar has a TV and a pool table, with a small area of seating for those wishing to take the weight off their feet, while in the saloon bar-cum-restaurant you will find an altogether different atmosphere. The seating is for the business of eating and relaxing in more comfort. The menu includes a selection from jacket potatoes through sandwiches, huffers and the main restaurant menu. Sunday roasts to à la carte choices are all available. This means all tastes can be catered for including vegetarians. I was drawn to the duck and crab specialities! Telephone: 01245 360487.

The Walk

① Turn right from the pub and left into Brook Hill. Walk down the road to cross the stream then turn left into Church Hill. After No 19 turn left onto a concrete path. After 50 yards go round a closed metal gate and continue on under the A130 to just before Sheepcotes Farm.

② Turn right and cross a two-plank bridge (we found the direction post hidden under the fir tree). Walk ahead with the hedge on your left, turn left and cross the track. Turn right and walk with the hedge on your right. At the bridge turn right and left to walk with the hedge on your left. Cross the next bridge and continue straight on with a hedge on the right to the road and footpath sign.

③ Turn right and walk downhill till you come to a footpath sign on your right. At this you turn left beside Kingswood then

go under a metal gate half right. Walk this green lane till you come to a bridge on your left. Turn right as indicated by the yellow arrow and walk to the left of the ditch to the steps and stile by the road. Cross with care to the steps and stile opposite. You are now on the golf course.

④ Turn left on a well marked grass track to walk parallel with the road passing two yellow waymarks and a stile with waymark, follow the signs till you come to a right turn which leads you out to the road. At the road cross and follow the direction post to a golf practice area. At a wire turn right through the gap in the hedge. You have entered a Plantation Zone. Keep just to the right of this till you come to a white painted fence. You are now looking for a very small gap in the hedge that enables you to exit the golf course on to the road by a footpath sign.

The path by Croxton Mill.

⑤ Cross the road to a byway sign opposite and enter the byway by a five-bar gate. This gravel downhill track gives good views. Pass a sign 'Ford 400 yards'. Ignore the stile and Nature Reserve sign on your right. At the next junction of footpaths turn right between two white posts. In a few minutes you reach Croxton Mill, the river and superb views of the weir pond and Croxton Mill Cottage. Cross the river and walk right up the road.

PLACES OF INTEREST NEARBY

Moulsham Mill, Parkway, Chelmsford, is an early 18th century watermill housing workshops and small craft businesses plus a cafe. Telephone: 01245 608200.

Chelmsford Cathedral is a 15th century building with links with the USAAF from their stay here from 1942–5. Guided tours available. Telephone: 01245 420100.

⑥ Turn right at the footpath sign and walk between wire fences. Go straight on at the stile and bridge along a hedged lane. Your route takes you past the fishing lakes, a line of pill boxes and many cricket bat willows. You cross two two-plank bridges before you reach a footpath sign. Turn right. Ignore the bridge on your left and go straight on to the river. Cross the river on a metal and concrete bridge and turn left. Walk through the gate and across the garden to the left of the house under a chestnut tree, to a kissing gate and footpath sign.

⑦ Go straight ahead over a stile and through the kissing gate. You will be walking on a tarred path over a lovely water meadow where horses often graze. This brings you out at the road in the centre of the village. Turn right and walk up the hill back to the White Hart.

Chatham Green
The Windmill Motor Inn

MAP: OS EXPLORER 183 (GR 716152)   **WALK 9**   **DISTANCE:** 4 MILES

DIRECTIONS TO START: TO THE SOUTH OF GREAT LEIGHS ON THE A131, CHATHAM GREEN IS CLEARLY MARKED AND THE APPROPRIATE TURN OFF TO THE WEST IS SHOWN BY A HIGH AND DISTINCTIVE SIGN MARKED 'WINDMILL RESTAURANT'. **PARKING:** PARK AT THE WINDMILL MOTOR INN BUT PLEASE ASK PERMISSION BEFORE LEAVING FOR YOUR WALK.

Chatham Green lies in a splendidly rural position to the north of the parish of Little Waltham. The windmill dated from around 1829 and with its adjacent bakehouse served the local farming community for over 70 years. In fact it became a focal point of village life and by 1904, when flour milling had stopped altogether, the owner Henry Challis was trading as a beer retailer.

A good part of this walk follows a particularly attractive section of the Essex Way. A visit to Little Leighs, with its old church and pretty cottages, is followed by peaceful country paths and moated Hyde Hall.

The Windmill Motor Inn

The Windmill Inn, as it was called, was in the ownership of Ridley's Brewery, but following the closure of the pub in 1993 various proposals were put by the brewers for future use of the site. Finally, to the delight of almost everybody, the present owners acquired the property and it has been restored in the style of the 19th century. It now offers excellent food and drinks for all tastes, and additionally seven double en suite bedrooms have been built in the roadhouse and stable block. The menu embraces large plates of pork, chicken or beef as well as imaginatively filled baguettes and jacket potatoes, like the delicious cajun chicken and cheese and bacon potatoes we tried the day we visited the area. At present, the pub is closed all day on Mondays. Telephone: 01245 361188.

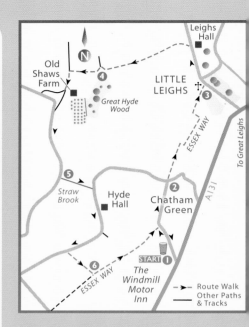

The Walk

① Coming from the pub, turn left along the lane to the little green on the corner. Turn right passing a row of pretty cottages. These dozen or so dwellings constitute the hamlet of Chatham Green.

② Cross a narrow lane into a track. Note the footpath sign bearing the legend 'Essex Way', which we are going to follow as far as Little Leighs church. The track reaches a stile and you then cross a pasture field to another stile. After crossing, follow the field edge with a hedge on your right. After about 500 yards the path turns sharp left and reaches the hedge at the other side of the field. Here a double Essex Way sign urges you to turn right with the hedge on your left. Soon you will reach a large fishing lake and the site of a new area of woodland named Church Broom Wood.

③ On reaching the lane turn left to pass Little Leighs church and some fine old cottages. Onward to Leighs Hall and turn left off the road on a concrete pathway uphill towards a wood. Pass two hedges on the right.

④ As a concrete track turns sharply to the left, keep on the right fork (west by a yellow arrow). Walk this rough path with a tall hedge on your left. At the end of the field

PLACES OF INTEREST NEARBY

At Rochester Farm, Great Leighs you will find the **Great Maze**. Set in wonderful Essex countryside this could be the world's largest maze: 4 miles of paths but only one path leads to the sunflower centre. Admission charge. Open 10 am to 7 pm. Telephone: 01245 361411.

The path near Little Leighs church.

locate a stile and plank bridge in the hedge opposite and cross. Turn left along the hedge for a few yards and cross another stile into a double-hedged lane. Soon you reach gardens on the right and a rough stile out onto the road. At Ivy Cottage ignore footpath signs and arrows but continue straight on down the farm road to a lane. Follow this delightfully quiet way for barely $1/2$ mile to reach a concrete path on your left.

⑤ This is Straw Brook and though barred to motorised traffic, it is used by local walkers and horse riders to connect the 350 yards between the two roads. On reaching

Hyde Hall Lane turn right past the moated hall. Pass the first footpath sign on the left and just past a house on your left turn left onto a path with a hedge and deep ditch on your left. Continue to a crossing hedge to cross a plank bridge by a white topped post. Now cross a small field in the same direction aiming for another white topped post.

⑥ Cross the hedge onto the Essex Way and turn left. From here walk this good path (about $3/4$ mile) into Chatham Green, finishing through a double-hedged green lane. Turn right when you reach the road back to the Windmill Motor Inn.

Shalford
The George

DIRECTIONS TO START: SHALFORD LIES IN THE PANT VALLEY NORTH-WEST OF BRAINTREE, ON THE B1053. **PARKING:** PARK AT THE GEORGE BUT PLEASE ASK FOR PERMISSION TO LEAVE YOUR CAR WHILE GOING ON THE STROLL.

Shalford village is crossed by the River Pant, which continues south behind the church and hall through a beautiful valley on its way to Bocking, later to change its name to the Blackwater. The village church with its 15th century tower is the treasure of Shalford but nearly everything else is a hundred years older. This is a lovely stroll through open countryside, climbing gently to Hunts Farm and then following quiet lanes and byways to return through Church End.

The George

The George is also an old building – about 500 years old, in fact. The real ale fixture is Greene King IPA with three or four guest beers to sample. The food is excellent, witnessed by the fact that throughout the week a good supply of regulars call in for their lunches. The blackboard menu is changed frequently but you will always find a choice of five or six main courses. We always enjoy the various pies which are served with a good selection of fresh vegetables. There is a pudding cabinet where you can take a look before you make your choice if you wish. Telephone: 01371 850207.

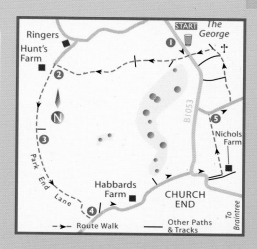

The Walk

① Cross the road from the pub and a few yards to the left follow a bridleway sign to join a defined path with a hedge on your

The view over the fishing lakes from point 5 of the walk.

The turkey at Habbards Farm

right. Enjoy the wide open sky as you climb for nearly ½ mile to a crossing path. Continue by the hedge, passing the old cottage Ringers away over to your right.

② ,Reach Hunt's Farm and a footpath sign and the unusual sight of a red arrow (public byway) pointing to your left. Your climb from the pub has been over 100 feet and this has brought you to the peace and solitude of the Essex countryside. The way goes south following the red arrow on level terrain with a good path between fields.

③ Keep left at the fork into the hedged lane (Park End Lane). When you come to a fence keep right and follow the track, swinging to right and left, out to the road passing some attractive old buildings.

④ At the road and a concrete public byway sign turn left. Walk through Shalford Church End passing on the way Habbards Farm where the coloured statue of a very large turkey decorates a barn. You reach the main road, B1053, and cross this with care to the right of the village sign. Follow downhill along a farm road to Nichol's Farm. A footpath sign points through a gate and over an unusual stile across the garden to a waymarked arrow and stile into a field at the rear. Continue in the same direction to the crest of a little hill. now walk on to a tall ash tree at a lane.

⑤ Turn right down the lane for 200 yards. Turn left at a footpath sign to follow the fence on your right and then a red brick wall to the church gates. Walk through the churchyard, bearing left to join a path out and in a few yards reach the George.

White Notley
The Plough

MAP: OS EXPLORER 183 & 195 (GR 773195)   **WALK 11**   **DISTANCE:** 3¾ MILES

DIRECTIONS TO START: WHITE NOTLEY LIES BETWEEN WITHAM AND BRAINTREE, ON THE UNNUMBERED ROAD THAT RUNS PARALLEL WITH THE B1018. THE PLOUGH IS ABOUT 1 MILE NORTH OF THE VILLAGE. **PARKING:** IN THE PLOUGH CAR PARK BUT PLEASE LET THE LANDLADY KNOW YOU ARE LEAVING YOUR CAR.

The Brain valley is made for walking. You start here with a descent to cross a golf course and the River Brain, and the next bit of excitement is crossing the Braintree-Witham railway line on the level crossing! Climbing out of the valley to reach Stubble's Farm, if you are like me, a lover of art, you may be drawn to look at Aubrey's wall. This is a unique wall built by C. H. Aubrey from old recycled materials and well worth a look. The Essex Way brings you back to Adams Wood, with its Conservation Walks, which may tempt you to explore. The return route gives you superb views back over the start of the walk.

The Plough

This is currently being run as a simple country pub. When you go through the door it is like entering someone's living room. There is a rear room with a pine feeling and this leads out to the conservatory and good views of the garden. The only food available is sandwiches that can be served plain or toasted. You will find a selection of Ridleys beers behind the bar, there is always IPA and at least one guest beer. Guinness, Strongbow, Stella Artois and Fosters make up the roll call. Telephone: 01376 327451.

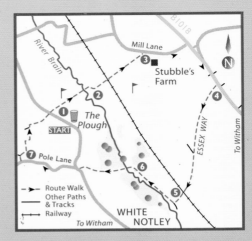

The Walk

① From the pub turn right and walk past the house next door, then right again to cross the stile beside the concrete footpath sign. Walk beside the fence and then straight ahead to a gate. Go over the stile and straight on again across the golf fairway. You are to go downhill under the power lines – you are aiming now for a humped river bridge. A yellow arrow here confirms you are right. You now go half right to pass another yellow arrow and pass to the left of a concrete mound numbered 009X009. Take the uphill track ahead.

② Quite soon you will spot a blue post and know to turn left and cross an earth bridge. You are heading for the railway crossing sign. (If you have continued on the track uphill to a wooden shed you have gone too far, go back and search again for the earth bridge.) Pass more blue marker posts and you will come to a stile, the railway line, and another stile. Your route ahead is on a well defined track. Go over a stile and on again over slightly rough ground to a fallen gate. Your route continues in the same direction with a hedge on your left. Walk under the electricity power lines to a stile.

③ Before your turn right into Mill Lane you may wish to stop and admire C.H. Aubrey's wall. Now walk about 1/3 mile up Mill Lane till you come to the junction with the B1018. Cross the road and walk down to the post box. Turn right and past the houses at Hawbush Green, which brings you to a path beside the B1018. Walk another 200 yards down the path till you nearly reach the pine factory. You now have to cross the sometimes busy road. You are leaving the road to join the second

PLACES OF INTEREST NEARBY

Cressing Temple Barns, built on what is now the B1018 between Witham and Braintree by warrior monks of the Knights Templar, are two most spectacular medieval timbered barns. They have been recently restored to their former glory and a 16th century paradise garden created. Telephone: 01376 584903 for more information.

The pond at Stubble's Farm.

footpath on your right. It is marked with a concrete footpath post with a green Essex Way sign attached.

④ This footpath is on the right of a hedge for about 10 yards. You then turn left over an earth bridge and immediately right again to walk with the hedge on your right. Yellow arrows confirm your route behind the barn to join a wide downhill track. Continue on this till you have gone through the tunnel under the railway line.

⑤ The public footpath is straight ahead with the hedge on your right. When you reach the crossing track turn right and walk this to Adams Wood.

⑥ Take the path left across a meadow to cross the Brain river on a small hump-backed bridge. Your route is marked as the John Ray Walk at this point. Turn half right and follow a path to a stile on your right. From this stile, bear left then with two further yellow arrows right to cross a two-plank bridge. Walk along the field edges and left out onto the road as directed by the many yellow arrows. Cross the road with care and turn left into Pole Lane. Walk past the first footpath sign and take the second on your right.

⑦ This footpath sign is one of the black and yellow varieties. After about 10 yards the John Ray Walk turns left and you continue right on a well walked path along the side of the fence. Three turns later go left between the fields and right over an earth bridge just before some bushes. Continue ahead and out onto the road. Cross half right back to the Plough.

Danbury
The Bell

MAP: OS EXPLORER 183 (GR 774053) **WALK 12** **DISTANCE:** 2 MILES

DIRECTIONS TO START: DANBURY IS ON THE A414 BETWEEN CHELMSFORD AND MALDON, AND ACCESSIBLE FROM THE A12 SOUTH OF BOREHAM. **PARKING:** AT THE BELL BUT PLEASE ASK THE LICENSEE BEFORE YOU SET OFF.

What a splendid place the village of Danbury is, sitting on the top of one of the most pronounced hills in Essex and surrounded by beautiful woodland and common and lakes. At the very top of the hill is the church, a fine building which must always have been too big for the parish numbers. In 1402, it is said, the Devil appeared in Danbury. At the same instant there chanced wind, thunder and lightning so that the highest part of the roof of the church was blown down and the chancel was rent and torn in pieces. The Devil took one of the bells and although it was dropped in Bell Hill Wood the Danbury men were most unwilling to ring the new bell which replaced it. Because of its situation, this stroll from Danbury involves some steeper paths but the effort is well worthwhile. The outward path leads through pastures and woodland, to return across Lingwood Common and Bell Hill.

The Bell

The Bell public house is down the hill towards Chelmsford opposite the grounds of the Palace. Here is a fine choice of draught beers. Young's Bitter and Special and Tetley's, to suit the taste of most. The cooked food too is invariably excellent, with the menu on the wall varying slightly each day but often repeating favourites. Liver and bacon is just one of these and can be had fried with chips or grilled with mashed potatoes. My wife's favourite is the home-made chicken and ham pie that comes with a delicious tasty gravy, chips and peas. The one-room premises are welcoming as well as friendly. In the summer a comfortable garden invites you. Telephone: 01245 222028.

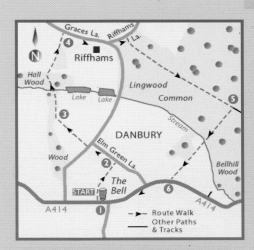

The path through Riffhams.

The Walk

① At the end of the car park from the Bell a concrete footpath sign points from the road along a twitten at the side of the pub garden. A twitten is a path through town or village houses which is only open to pedestrians. This particular one crosses an estate road and proceeds downhill to Elm Green Lane, and another concrete sign.

② Turn left down the lane and at the bottom cross over the road to a stile. Over the stile continue on under a sycamore tree on a lovely path in a pasture field, part of the grounds of Riffhams, a large house over to your right.

③ When you reach a wood cross the stile by a yellow arrow waymark and enter the path which bears right uphill. Shortly leave the wood and bear right past farm

PLACES OF INTEREST NEARBY

Danbury church is well worth a visit. Among the many items of interest, look for the pews ornamented with lions and dragons.

The grounds of Riffhams.

buildings, walking uphill with the hedge on your right. Just to the left of a gate cross a stile into a country lane (Graces Lane).

④ Turn right along the lane, passing the imposing gates of Riffhams, to reach a road junction. Bear left up Riffhams Chase. Soon turn right into Lingwood Common. There is a concrete bridleway sign. Keep on the main track going south-eastwards. This is a famous pathway on which many notable feet have progressed down the years including Sir Walter Scott who resided at the nearby Griffin Inn where he wrote part of *Queenhoo Hall*.

⑤ Just short of the top of Bell Hill there is a significant track to the right going fairly steeply downhill. There is a post at the beginning of the path with blue arrows on the east side and a green Wildside Walk sign. Go downhill with this path. After the path starts to climb, bridleway signs show the route up to the Street in Danbury. It is quite a pull up but fear not.

⑥ When you reach the Street turn right (all downhill now), passing Elm Green back to the pub.

Bicknacre
The Brewers Arms

MAP: OS EXPLORER 183 (GR 788022)	**WALK 13**	DISTANCE: 1½ MILES

DIRECTIONS TO START: BICKNACRE IS TO THE SOUTH OF DANBURY, ON THE B1418, THE BREWERS ARMS BEING ½ MILE SOUTH OF THE VILLAGE. **PARKING:** AVAILABLE AT THE BREWERS ARMS WITH THE LANDLORD'S PERMISSION.

Bicknacre has grown up on the site of an ancient Augustan priory – hence the 'Priory Garage' that you passed on your way to the start! There is, alas, nothing of the ancient ruins to be seen from the village these days. You will be walking partly on footpaths and bridleways and partly through the Thrift Wood Nature Reserve, giving a pleasant mixture of open agricultural land and well enclosed woods. For such a short stroll you do get a feeling of being away from it all, in an area that has probably changed little since the days of the priors.

The Brewers Arms

This long public house is split into several bar areas. One large old brick fireplace dominates the entrance, and another the left-hand end wall. In the winter you may well be greeted by log fires, while in the summer you may choose to use the large pub garden. The menu includes sandwiches, ploughman's and jacket potatoes, plus a range of cooked food from burgers to steaks and in between lasagne, fish and chips, and the ever popular steak and kidney pudding. To wash down your meal you will find on hand pump four or five cask ales; Greene King IPA and Abbott are the regular beers plus three guest beers. There are at least three lagers including 1664 and Strongbow cider on hand pump plus a bottled cider. The pub is not open on Tuesday lunch time but you will be well served every other mid-day. Telephone: 01245 224061.

The Walk

① From the pub, cross the road from the car park near the recycling centre to the bridleway sign and walk down the gravel track edged with houses. This soon becomes very rural.

② A path joins from your left – note this as you will use it on your way home. About 10 yards further on turn right at the bridleway sign. This is richly decorated with a St Peter's Way sign and a Wildside Walk badge. You soon come to a crossing footpath marked with a double footpath sign, a bench seat and three posts spaced across the bridleway. Turn right here and enter Thrift Wood Nature Reserve.

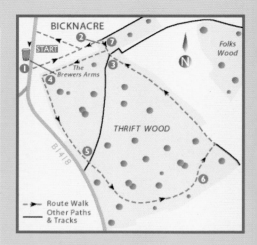

③ Cross the earth bridge and walk right across a clearing. A ditch soon appears on your right and you are walking through woods down its right-hand side.

④ As the path reaches the end of the wood it turns left and you will find yourself walking along the backs of gardens on a still wide woodland path. The path swings slightly left and you come out into more open woodland.

⑤ When you come to a crossing track turn right and come out into a clearing by a gate through which you can see the traffic on the B1418. This is the western end of the public footpath that crosses this reserve. From the centre of the clearing turn left, then right at the Wildside Walk courtesy footpath sign. This path takes you south-east. Cross a faint track and go straight ahead.

⑥ When you come to a wooded area ignore the path to the right, which is very overgrown, and turn left to an open area with small silver birch trees. You now reach

A footpath junction at point 7 on the walk.

a main track. Turn left along this. Fork right and right again to a grassy clearing. Turn right and find a log seat. Just a few yards right again and you will see on your left the exit from the reserve to the southern end of the bridleway. A short series of steps brings you down to the bridleway, turn left along the wide all-weather path.

⑦ Before long you reach the seat and pass the three posts you passed earlier. Make your way back to the T junction, turn left and look for the path you noted on the way out. It is marked with a blue arrow on a white post. Bear right along this bridleway. The grass edged track soon becomes gravel and you have reached the road. Turn left to pass St Andrew's church and you soon rejoin your car at the pub.

PLACES OF INTEREST NEARBY

The RHS Garden at **Hyde Hall**, Rettendon consists of 8 acres of landscaped hill top garden, fish ponds and a cafe. Telephone: 01245 400256.

South Woodham Ferrers
The Whalebone Inn

MAP: OS EXPLORER 175 (GR 799979)	WALK 14	DISTANCE: 1½ MILES

DIRECTIONS TO START: COMING NORTH-EAST ON THE A132, AT THE SHAW FARM ROUNDABOUT GO AHEAD TO THE NEXT ROUNDABOUT. TAKE THE THIRD EXIT, OLD WICKFORD ROAD. **PARKING:** PARK ON THE ROAD NEAR THE WHALEBONE INN IF IT IS CLOSED. IF IT IS OPEN HAVE A WORD WITH THE PUBLICAN TO CONFIRM YOU CAN LEAVE THE CAR WHILE YOU DO THE WALK.

A walk along the banks of a stream brings you to the Woodham Fenn Reserve, which is managed by Essex Wildlife Trust and South Woodham Ferrers Town Council. This wild and unspoiled area is a Site of Special Scientific Interest and a wetland of international importance. Strangers to the area will be surprised to find this large parcel of untouched creekside so near to one of Essex's new towns. In fact, the area looks much as it did when there were just 950 residents to the town, not the 20,000 or more it currently caters for. Your way over the railway line leads you along the banks of Fenn Creek, where you walk on mown grass tracks and can enjoy the range of butterflies and insects making busy journeys from plant to plant along your route.

The Whalebone Inn

The outside of this attractive pub is painted pale pink and in the summer it is garlanded with flowers. The children's play area is to the left of the car park whilst on the right is a large patio and grassed outdoor eating area. The old beamed interior gives the feeling of space with side rooms that just encourage you to enter and explore further. The large function room makes a bright modern addition. The chef's chalk board carries a wide range of specials so this with the regular choice of hot favourites will more than replace the energy used up on the walk. The big all day breakfast with two of everything would suit the hungriest of walkers whilst those in a hurry will find a suitable snack in the wide range of jacket potatoes, sandwiches and baguettes. Amongst the more unusual fillings are bacon and stilton, and smoked salmon and cream cheese. Those making the visit to celebrate a really special anniversary may choose to ask for the a la carte menu. The pub boasts four real ales, Greene King, Tetley, John Smith and Marstons Pedigree. Strongbow cider is available on draught. Children are welcome in the bar to eat. For more information ring 01245 320231.

The Walk

① Leave the pub by continuing further down the old Wickford Road. Just after the gates of Fenn Farm turn left at the concrete footpath sign to walk beside the stream. The path takes you over a three-plank bridge to cross a stile and climb a few steps uphill to cross a rather awkwardly placed crash barrier. Cross this busy road with care.

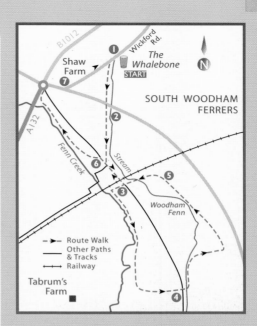

② At the footpath sign opposite cross another easier crash barrier and stile. Walk straight on with the stream on your left and you will very soon join a mown track. Ignore the bridge on your left and walk straight on to a kissing gate and railway crossing. Cross the single track railway line and go through the kissing gate on the far side.

③ Turn right with the mown track that

PLACES OF INTEREST NEARBY

Marsh Farm Country Park, Marsh Farm Road. Just follow the brown signs across town to this working farm adjoining the river. Telephone: 01245 321552.

Battlesbridge Antiques Centre is just about 4 miles away to the south-west. There are over 70 dealers of antiques and crafts for you to visit clustered round the one site. Telephone: 01268 575000.

Woodham Fenn Nature Reserve.

runs beside the railway line. At the creek turn left, still on the track. Now follows a pleasant creekside walk. The farm you can see across the fields to your right is Tabrum's Farm. As the track leaves the creekside follow it across the meadow. Two logs help you across the stream to join the main gravel track.

④ Turn right and follow the public footpath. Cross the stream ahead on a concrete bridge. Turn left and take the path that leads in front of the water treatment plant. Just uphill past the treatment centre turn left on another grass track leading north-west. You may wish to take a rest on the lovely bench. Walk straight on, ignore the path to your right. You are heading back to the railway.

⑤ Just before the hedge as the track turns right you turn left, climb over a grass mound and head for a wooden bridge ahead. Walk straight on to rejoin the main track and turn right to re-cross the railway line.

⑥ Take the mown track on your left heading towards a bench. Ignore the left turn and go ahead under the power line. The track swings right, left and right again as you head for a kissing gate and farm gate by Shaw Farm roundabout.

⑦ Turn right and walk the tarred path to cross the roundabout in Ferrers Road. Head for the bridleway sign on your right and turn left, this narrow path soon becomes the old Wickford Road and you retrace your steps to the pub.

Wickham St Paul
The Victory Inn

MAP OS EXPLORER196 (GR 831364)	**WALK 15**	**DISTANCE:** 3 MILES

DIRECTIONS TO START: LYING BETWEEN THE A131 AND B1058, WICKHAM ST PAUL IS EQUIDISTANT FROM SUDBURY AND HALSTEAD. THE VICTORY INN IS ON THE GREEN. **PARKING:** ON THE ROAD BY THE VICTORY INN.

In a delightfully peaceful setting, Wickham St Paul has an old village green, and the church, with Wickham Hall by its side, has been owned by St Paul's Cathedral for over 1,000 years. The church has a Tudor tower and part of the nave is 12th century. From the green, you pass the church and then stroll along field paths and by the little stream that runs near the village, to return by Butler's Hall Farm.

The Victory Inn

The Victory is on the village green, with space and tranquillity in abundance. The real ales are Adnams, Greene King and the delightful Nethergate as well as varying guest beers. Eating is extremely well catered for with extensive and varied blackboard items. It would seem that customers come from far and wide to savour the food and drink. We have eaten here several times and we are sure like us you will be amazed with the size of the plates for fish and chips. Our cod at first seemed small till we realised it was itself about the length of a normal pub plate and it had come with a side bowl of chips and an excellent salad that included red currants and strawberries in its garnish, a ready made pudding we felt. There is also a mid week menu for young at heart customers; this offers excellent value for money which will we are sure save you even thinking of eating again that day. Telephone 01787 269364.

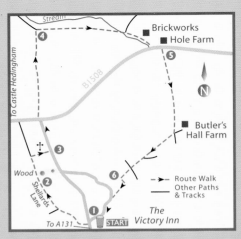

The Walk

① From the pub cross the road by the green at a 'No Through Road' sign and turn right into Shellards Lane, passing a pond on your right. Caution, the pond is marked 'deep water'. At the end of the lane just past a thatched cottage continue in the same line into a large field. Ahead a section of woodland projects from the road.

② At the left edge of this woodland you should aim for the field edge and cross through a hedge by a stile and plank bridge. Follow a ditch on your right and come close to the church. At the field corner leave the path. The locals use this access to the church by turning right along the fence to the church and you can follow their footsteps to the road. You may wish to visit the church if it is open.

③ Afterwards turn left along the road to

The village pond.

The start of the walk.

the T junction. Now join the path across the road at a concrete public footpath sign, along a concrete track almost due north for 850 yards. After an open section there is a hedge on the right and the path goes downhill. After 15 yards, before the bottom, look for a gap in the hedge on the right.

④ Turn right through the gap and walk across this field to find another gap and an earth bridge through the hedge. If the path has been reinstated walk straight over the field to the stream, or follow the field edge to left and right to the same point. Cross the stream on an earth bridge and turn right into and through the wood following the orange arrow. Follow the orange arrow to the brickworks (here they manufacture simulated antique bricks). Past the works turn left and then right to the road. (Careful, it can be busy). Turn left for a few yards up this road.

⑤ Join a bridleway, turning right off the road up a farm track (fairly steep). This leads after barely ½ mile to Butler's Hall Farm. Turn right at the end of the buildings and turn left, aiming for a single bushy tree down by the stream side. A few yards to the left of this tree is a plank bridge with a yellow arrow which you cross and head uphill towards a telegraph pole.

⑥ Past the pole turn left with an arrow and soon reach another arrow pointed through the hedge. Follow the defined path through this field to reach a lane. Follow the lane to the left and soon reach the Victory Inn.

PLACES OF INTEREST NEARBY
In Halstead go to the **Townsend Mill Antiques Centre** in the Causeway, one of the largest antiques centres in Essex. This old mill was one of Courtaulds first silk weaving factories, now over 75 dealers display antiques and collectibles. Telephone: 01787 474451. Bed and breakfast is available in the adjoining Mill House, full of character and a wealth of nostalgia.

Little Braxted
The Green Man

MAP: OS EXPLORER 183 (GR 849130)   **WALK 16**   **DISTANCE:** 4 MILES

DIRECTIONS TO START: FROM WITHAM PASS UNDER THE A12. TURN LEFT OVER THE BLUE MILLS BRIDGE AND CARRY ON UPHILL TO WICKHAM BISHOPS. ON REACHING THE VILLAGE TURN LEFT ALONG TIPTREE ROAD AND LEFT UP KELVEDON ROAD TO THE GREEN MAN. **PARKING:** AT THE GREEN MAN, PLEASE ASK PERMISSION BEFORE SETTING OUT ON THE WALK.

Little Braxted parish lies south of the River Blackwater and includes to the south a slice of Wickham Bishops. In the village the church which is only 45 feet long stands beside a timbered house and a huge thatched barn which has been there for 400 years. Inside the church are decorations left by a vicar of the 19th century, created by his own brushes and paints! Just across the green opposite the pub lies Braxted Place, an imposing red house with, attached to the end by the footpath, a tiny chapel which is worth a look if open. The walk is firstly downhill to the river, in open country with long views over Witham. Then you go across the golf course to Wickham church and through the footpaths and twittens of Wickham Bishops, another of the hilltop villages of Essex. These footpaths reveal the hidden charms of some of the extensive gardens in the village.

The Green Man

The Green Man has for many years been a fine example of a 'Ridleys pub' serving the regular beers as well as the seasonal varieties brewed by regional breweries, of which Ridleys is the best Essex example. The present tenants at the Green Man have carried on the tradition of their predecessors with splendid home-cooked foods. There is a sign outside the building 'Haggis a speciality' and so it is, with traditional main course meals and haggis baguettes! Telephone: 01621 891659.

The Walk

① Leave the Green Man, going to the left. Soon fork left, signposted Witham, by the Old School House. There are considerable views ahead over the Blackwater valley. Pass Hales Farm, the house built near to the road, and then go past Sewells Farm to a corner of the road.

② Turn left by a concrete public footpath sign and follow the concrete path round to the right. The path bends to the left into a wooded area and soon turns right on a narrow path.

③ Cross a stile and turn left following a reinstated path going south past a large modern house with an extensive garden. At the end turn right and join Ishams Chase near the River Blackwater, to the road at Blue Mills.

④ Cross the busy road with care and walk over the golf course in a south-easterly direction aiming uphill for a stile in the

The giant chestnut tree near the village pub.

PLACES OF INTEREST NEARBY

Chelmer Cruises, Paper Mill Lock, Little Baddow, Chelmsford operate cruises along the **Chelmer and Blackwater Canal** providing a unique view of rural Essex. There are public trips on the barge *Victoria* operating at weekends. Open April to October. Telephone: 01245 225520.

The delightful village sign.

facing hedge. Continue in the same direction diagonally over a grassy field to a gap in the hedge opposite. Walk with a wood on your left and follow over stiles to and through Glebe Farm steading and to Mope Lane.

⑤ Turn right uphill for 500 yards. Here turn left passing Wickham Bishops church and Church Green. Fork right at Blacksmiths Lane. Cross the main road by the Mitre pub and enter Great Totham Road.

⑥ Turn left at a concrete public footpath sign and continue on this path for barely a mile, crossing a road on the way, to turn left up a road for a few yards. Turn left off this road at a public footpath sign. Cross a stile and walk by lovely gardens to Mountains Road. Turn left for a few yards then right through a twitten, over a narrow road and through a thicket, keeping straight on back to the Green Man.

Colne Engaine
The Five Bells

MAP: OS EXPLORER195 (GR 851303) **WALK 17** **DISTANCE:** 3 MILES

DIRECTIONS TO START: COLNE ENGAINE LIES NORTH OF THE RIVER COLNE, AND THE A1124, BETWEEN HALSTEAD AND COLCHESTER. **PARKING:** PARK AT THE FIVE BELLS BUT PLEASE DON'T FORGET TO ASK PERMISSION AT THE BAR TO LEAVE YOUR CAR WHILE GOING FOR YOUR WALK.

Of all four Colne villages – Earls, White, Wakes, and Engaine – the last is probably the most attractive as it is in a secluded position away from busy roads, on a hill commanding views of the Colne valley. The church is not far short of the highest point and its brick battlements make a good landmark. The best of it is the handsome stepped porch, excellent brickwork in the traditional Essex manner. Leaving Colne Engaine to walk down to the River Colne, you climb on a good grass track towards Over Hall, and a wonderful view over the valley, before returning to explore this lovely village.

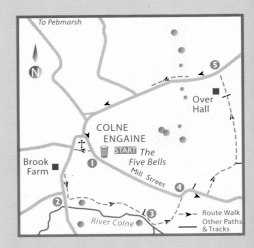

The Five Bells

A real village local that can supply the needs of most people, residents and visitors alike. A freehouse and therefore able to stock any beer, when we visited the choice was from Timothy Taylors Landlord, Greene King IPA, or Nethergate Autumn. At lunchtime most of the customers are eating as well as drinking, and the range of dishes is such as to tempt everyone. Just to mention a few: chicken Wellington, sizzling stir fry, curries, a choice of ten starters, and lots of cold and hot desserts. All this may be inadvisable if you plan to walk afterwards but is probably just the thing if your walk precedes lunch! Telephone 01787 224166.

The Walk

① Leave the pub to turn right up the road. At the church turn left at a concrete public footpath sign. The way passes the front of the church and continues through the yard to the road. Turn left and walk downhill out of the village passing Brook Farm. On your left is a high banked field. The edge of this is not a public path but locals walk on this and you may wish to follow them.

② Towards the bottom of the field a plank bridge from the road leads on to the path near a public footpath sign. Follow the path eastwards by the side of a wood, and at the end of the wood a short section crosses an open field to a stile. Ignore this stile and continue on to cross a plank bridge leading to the river side.

③ Cross the dismantled railway and

Colne Engaine church.

follow the river, bearing left to a long bridge. Ignore this bridge and bear left to

Mill Lane, Colne Engaine.

the old railway line. Cross straight over the line down to a stile marked with an arrow. Cross this and another stile to a field edge. Walk up with a hedge and ditch on your right to reach a road near Mill Cottage.

④ Follow the road past a mill. Just before Millbrooks Farm turn left into a pasture field crossing two stiles. At the end of the field turn right at a stile to continue in the same direction but now with the hedge on your left. Follow this hedge turning right. Cross into a small field and bear left to a stile which you cross to climb on a good grass track by the hedge. Having gained the height look back for a great view over the valley. You come to Over Hall – slightly to the left cross a stile. Look to the left for the statue! Resuming your stroll towards the Hall, after a few yards turn right into a wood. Immediately turn left out of the wood between buildings on to a drive. The drive passes an intriguing brick wall with several curved sections before leading to the road.

⑤ Turn left downhill, passing Over Hall and at the bottom of the hill a footpath crosses the road. Continue on the road but in a few yards a courtesy path follows closely the line of the road on your right. When this finishes near some cottages you continue on the road, reaching Colne Engaine at Green Farm Road. At the village green turn left into Church Street leading on to Mill Lane and the Five Bells.

PLACES OF INTEREST NEARBY

The **Colne Valley Railway**, Yeldham Road, Castle Hedingham, provides steam train rides on a section of the former Colne Valley line. Buffet car, souvenir shop, riverside and grassland picnic area; luxury Pullman restaurant train. Admission includes rides. Steam days each Sunday and Bank Holiday. Telephone 01787 461174.

Gosfield Lake resort off Church Road, Gosfield is a 36 acre lake which has water skiing and fishing, overlooked by a picnic area. Licensed restaurant and snack bar. Admission charge. Open April to September. Telephone 01787 475043.

Pebmarsh
The King's Head

DIRECTIONS TO START: PEBMARSH IS SIGNPOSTED OFF THE A131 BETWEEN HALSTEAD AND SUDBURY. **PARKING:** PARK AT THE KING'S HEAD; ASK THE LANDLORD BEFORE LEAVING YOUR CAR WHILST YOU WALK.

Pebmarsh is a gem of a village, lying in that glorious area of Essex countryside north-east of Halstead. The parish can boast several Tudor farms and houses, but the church has many older treasures including a brass dating from the 1300s. There are believed to be only about 16 surviving from this early date and this one depicts Sir William Fitzralph who fought in the wars of Edward I against the Scots. The church is mostly 14th century, there is a beautiful doorway with four animal heads, a 15th century bell and a 500 year old pulpit. This lovely stroll takes you through woodland and beside fishing lakes, where the swans, ducks and other birds will entertain you as you go. More woodland and field paths bring you back to continue exploring Pebmarsh village.

The King's Head

The King's Head is a fine old building with an oak-beamed interior dating from 1470. Usually these have a nautical connection. Greene King IPA is usually on tap as well as three constantly changing guest beers. Cooked food is on the menu both at lunchtime and in the evening. The surprisingly large selection of dishes include regular fare and a number of Mexican dishes. The day we were there a party of eight including two young children were enjoying a mixed meal from simple chips plus lunches for the younger members of the party to exotic fish and steaks for older members. We went in very cold and wet having been caught in a downpour on our way back from the walk. We were impressed with the friendly atmosphere and the warming food. Telephone 01787 269306.

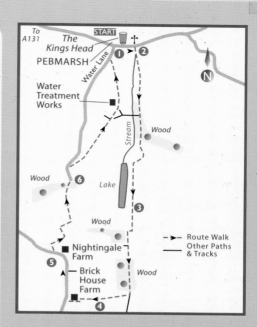

The Walk

① Leaving the pub turn left through the village. Soon you will pass the quaint little petrol station and a tiny post office and stores. The church is well worth a visit.

② Opposite the church turn right off the main road and walk to the end. Continue in this direction following a footpath sign and waymark into a wood. The route keeps mainly to the left in the wood. Ignore a yellow arrow pointing downhill to the right, later following the path down to the right and out to the end of the wood. Follow south through the valley. A long fishing lake has been constructed in recent years which is nearly ½ mile long. As this does not appear even on the latest Ordnance Survey maps do not be confused,

the path line is still the same! Follow the lake south but some 25 yards higher.

③ At the end of the lake the path bears right down to a woodside and left along it. Proceed on this path by the wood across a field and into the next wood, still going south. Pass two separate yellow arrows inviting you to the right. At the end of the wood you enter, a third arrow is the one to follow over a bridge and uphill with a hedge on your left to Brick House Farm.

④ Cross a stile, turn left for 15 yards and turn right again uphill to another stile into an orchard. At a five-barred gate join a

PLACES OF INTEREST NEARBY

The **East Anglian Railway Museum** at Chappel Station is a working museum of 100 years of railway engineering and architecture. Telephone: 01206 242524.

The village petrol station and post office in Pebmarsh.

little lane and follow it to the right.

⑤ Barely ¹/₂ mile on turn left at a sharp bend by Nightingale Farm and very soon cross a stile on the right into a field. Follow the path round the field edge keeping the hedge closely to your left, and cross the stile on your left out of the field into a large arable field. Follow the path northwards to reach a patch of woodland. A track goes through this which you follow, turning right downhill.

⑥ At the end turn left up a farm track and turn right at the top. Do not continue on the track at this point but follow the waymark to the right of the hedge going north-eastwards across a field to a water treatment works. Here take the path to the left through the woods and by a field edge path with a hedge on your right reach a little road (Water Lane). Turn right along this for the last 350 yards into Pebmarsh village.

Mundon
The White Horse

MAP: OS EXPLORER 176 (GR 870025)   **WALK 19**   **DISTANCE:** 2½ MILES

DIRECTIONS TO START: FROM MALDON TAKE THE FAMBRIDGE ROAD B1018 SOUTH. BEYOND THE ROYAL OAK PUB TURN LEFT AT A CROSSROADS ALONG BLIND LANE. AT THE NEXT CROSSING TURN RIGHT INTO MUNDON VILLAGE. **PARKING:** YOU MAY PARK IN THE WHITE HORSE CAR PARK. PLEASE ASK PERMISSION TO LEAVE YOUR CAR WHILE DOING THE WALK OR IF THERE IS NO ONE THERE LEAVE A NOTE THROUGH THE DOOR TO ADVISE.

The little parish of Mundon contains only a small population, a handful of farms and a row of cottages centred around the White Horse – but it has a beautiful little church which is a highlight of this walk. The north porch is spectacular and the church, now sadly redundant but still cared for, has a weatherboarded, timber-framed tower. This is good walking country and the St Peters Way passes through the village on its way from Purleigh to Maylandsea. Nothing so strenuous for today though, just a pleasant stroll through a small but historic part of Essex.

The White Horse

Popular with the villagers, in many ways the pub is the social centre of the village, while remaining friendly to visitors. The building is 400 years old and was originally two cottages either side of the back to back fireplace. The pub sign by the road is unusual, showing a white horse on one side and on the other its upside down reflection. Real ales include Greene King IPA and three or four guest beers to tempt the drinker. For snacks a good range of baked potatoes, ploughman's, and sandwiches are on offer. I well remember the prawn jacket with blue stilton which I enjoyed so much at the White Horse. The range of reasonably priced meals is extensive – chicken, mushroom and ham pie, 'Ham it up' gammon, with two eggs and chips, curry of the week, steaks, and steak and kidney pie are just a few of the selection, and a choice of seven desserts to follow. Above the bar is a huge collection of hats. Telephone: 01621 740276.

The Walk

① From the pub turn left along the main road. At West Chase turn left following a concrete public footpath sign and follow the track between two fields to a metalled road. Continue onward and turn right past Mundon Hall. Pass a lily pond on your left into a grassy area and turn left to the church. This was made redundant in 1970 and leased to Friends of Churches in 1975. The building is Grade I Listed, mainly 14th century and however you arrive there it is all peace and tranquillity – certainly far from the madding crowd. After your visit retrace your steps to the pond and follow

Mundon Hall Farm

the road northwards to the stile on the corner.

② Cross the stile to a waymark at the field corner. Turn left along a field edge with a hedge on your right. At the end of the field cross a stile and bridge, briefly turning right and then left with a hedge on your left.

St Mary's church.

Continue to a concrete public footpath sign by a road.

③ Turn left by a house called 'The Orchards'. Turn left up Vicarage Lane. At the corner of the lane spot a white gate.

④ Turn right with the yellow arrow through the gate and follow to a stile with a hedge on your right. Cross a stile on to the side of the main road. Now turn left for a few yards and you are back at the White Horse.

PLACES OF INTEREST NEARBY

The **Maeldune Centre**, Plume Building, Market Hill/High Street, Maldon, has a 42 foot long embroidery displayed in its new heritage centre, celebrating the 1,000th anniversary of the Battle of Maldon. Admission charge. Open seven days a week, April to September, 10.30 am to 4.30 pm. Telephone: 01621 851628.

Henny Street
The Swan

MAP: OS EXPLORER 195 (GR 879385)	WALK 20	DISTANCE: 3 MILES

DIRECTIONS TO START: HENNY STREET IS ON THE WEST BANK OF THE RIVER STOUR BETWEEN SUDBURY AND BURES ON AN UNNUMBERED SIDE ROAD. SO COMING FROM BURES TAKE THE ROAD NORTH THROUGH LAMARSH. FROM SUDBURY TAKE THE ROAD SOUTH THROUGH MIDDLETON. TAKE CARE AS ALL THE APPROACH ROADS ARE RATHER NARROW. **PARKING:** PARK ON THE ROAD OPPOSITE THE SWAN BUT PLEASE LET THE LANDLORD KNOW YOU ARE THERE.

This area beside the river and up into the parishes of Little Henny and Great Henny in places appears untouched by time. You will find old green lanes that seem to have sunk into the surrounding countryside. From the valley bottom you climb some 150 feet to Great Henny church, where the views towards Sudbury and Little Cornard are lovely. The church has been described as 'not an important building' but nevertheless it is full of history. The altar of the children's chapel is said to be made from a chest thought to have come from Italy in the 16th century. In the 18th century Jacob Brome was rector for no less than 57 years! The return walk is on quiet country lanes passing Tymperly Farm and Little Hickbush.

The Swan

Standing as it does on the banks of the River Stour, this is a good place to visit on a warm summer day. There is a tiny pontoon where boats trip along the river. The pub is divided into bars and restaurant by large oak beams. There is a very large blackboard menu; when I visited choices included steak pie, turkey, ham and mushroom pie, mixed meat curry, fish dishes, cheesy leek and potato bake, and Sunday roasts. All meals are served with fresh vegetables or chips. You may just want a light snack like sandwiches, ploughman's, or jumbo sausages in a roll. Pudding choices include Eve's pudding, and steamed suet pudding with jam or syrup. There is also a restaurant with a separate menu. A wine list is available. Beers include Greene King IPA and Abbott plus, there is normally a guest beer on hand pump. Cider lovers will find a choice of Strongbow and Scrumpy Jack. Telephone 01787 269238 for more information.

The Walk

① From the pub walk north-east up the road till you come to the junction with the road signed Middleton. Turn left and walk past Henny Cottage on a narrow road that soon begins to take you uphill. As the road turns sharp right look for a bridleway sign on your left.

② Turn left along this bridleway, but not before you note the views behind you. You soon come to a little brook. Cross this on the three stepping stones placed for your use. You will soon come to a bridleway sign and road junction.

③ Turn right. You are now walking toward the church tower at the top of the hill. Pass a concrete Public Bridleway sign and enjoy the super views as you make your way on to pass Applecroft Farm on your right. As the road turns right, you turn left on a grass track with a hedge on your left. As the hedge ends, turn right with the uphill track toward the church. Turn left at

PLACES OF INTEREST NEARBY

Sudbury town has many interesting places to visit including the swimming pool centre, the Quay theatre, and the lovely disused railway line walk north out of town alongside the river and water meadows. The Lovejoy railway line ends at Sudbury station itself.

Boat trips are available to the Swan on Sundays and Bank Holidays, run in conjunction with the River Stour Trust. The trips pick up by the Quay Theatre in Sudbury and make their way via the new lock, provided partly with a lottery grant, along the River Stour. En route to the pub they pass 10 to 15 barges sunk in the war. The boats allow you time for a meal before they take you on the return trip. Telephone: 01787 269238.

Delightful cottages near the start of the walk.

the concrete public footpath into the churchyard. Pass the church and the pretty flint cottages to the right of the gate. Two yellow arrows confirm your route. You are to walk downhill on part of the St Edmund Way and Stour Valley Path.

④ At the direction post you have joined the road. Turn left walking on the road. At the first junction take Lamarsh Road which is straight on. At the sign 'Hickbush Only' turn left on the road and walk downhill.

⑤ At the concrete footpath sign turn left and walk along the crop divide on a well defined path to the public footpath sign at the road ahead.

⑥ On reaching the road turn right and walk downhill to the T junction. Turn left and walk past Street Farm and back to the pub.

Little Totham
The Swan

MAP: OS EXPLORER 183 (GR 890117)	**WALK 21**	DISTANCE: 4 MILES

DIRECTIONS TO START: FROM THE B1022 MALDON TO COLCHESTER ROAD NEAR THE COMPASSES IN GREAT TOTHAM, DRIVE EAST PAST PLAINS FARM AND TURN RIGHT AT THE STREET AT LITTLE TOTHAM. **PARKING:** AT THE SWAN, EITHER BY THE ROAD OR AT THE REAR. PLEASE OBTAIN PERMISSION FROM THE LANDLORD.

The villagers at Little Totham live in a cosy group of houses round the pub and post office a mile north of the hall and church. Part of the hall is 500 years old. Close by is a lily pond, very pretty in the summer but not quite on the Monet scale! The composition is engulfed in trees – poplars, pines, and chestnuts. A magnificent Norman doorway admits you to the church and the ironwork of the doors is a fine representation of the smiths' work of the 12th and 13th century. This very pleasant stroll across farmland takes you through the charming hamlet of Totham Hill Green before turning east back to the start and the inviting Swan pub.

The Swan

The Swan is not so old as the church but still goes back to the 16th century. It was originally a lovely cottage set back behind a walled garden. The lounge is very comfortable, with oak beams. The beers are most varied with usually five on offer, perhaps stemming from the beer festival which the landlord holds each June. The blackboard menu normally includes a couple of starters, four main courses and some puddings. This is changed on a regular basis. When we were last there we tried a pasta dish that included tomatoes and fine strips of beef in a delicious sauce. This had been finished under the grill with melted cheese. A regular menu of standard pub dishes is also available. Telephone: 01621 892689.

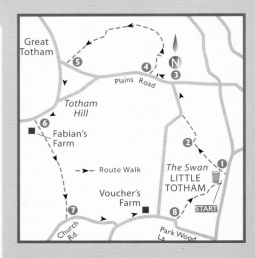

The Walk

① Right behind the pub a public footpath leads through a thicket north west by the south of the village. Recently the path had become rather overgrown but with a combination of council work and the efforts of walkers it is now in excellent shape.

② Coming into the open cross a footbridge and walk on to Office Farm. Pass on to a metalled farm track. To your right are the quaintly named Totham Plains. Carry straight on.

③ Reaching a road (Plains Road) turn left.

PLACES OF INTEREST NEARBY

Layer Marney Tower nearby is a magnificent example of Tudor architecture, incorporating the tallest Tudor gatehouse in Britain. You may climb to the top of the tower, explore the church and meet the farm animals. Admission charge. Open April to October every day except Saturday, 12 to 5 pm. Telephone: 01206 330784.

④ Ignore a bridleway sign but just before Plains Farm turn right at a concrete public footpath sign over a stile. Continue in this direction over two more stiles to join a bridleway after 350 yards. Turn left and after 400 yards cross a footbridge and turn left to walk west out to a road at Totham Hill Green.

⑤ Turn right and left round the corner and walk on south through this delightful hamlet past the green to turn right towards Fabian's Farm.

⑥ Turn left on a footpath and walk down with a hedge on your right and beyond that Foresters Golf Course.

⑦ Turn left when you reach a road and walk for ³/₄ mile past Vouchers Farm.

⑧ Turn left along a footpath following a stream on your right. Local doggy walkers use alternative routes but you should keep going north-east to the road just off the village centre. When you reach a road turn left for the few yards back to the pub.

Messing
The Old Crown Inn

MAPS: OS EXPLORER 183 & 184 (GR 899190) · **WALK 22** · **DISTANCE:** 4 MILES

DIRECTIONS TO START: MESSING LIES TO THE EAST OF KELVEDON, OFF THE A12.
PARKING: IT IS POSSIBLE TO PARK AT THE OLD CROWN INN OR IN THE VILLAGE STREET.
IF THE FORMER PLEASE OBTAIN THE PERMISSION OF THE LANDLORD BEFORE SETTING
OUT ON THE STROLL.

Messing is a peaceful little place where the church walls carry fragments of Roman bricks and many of the cottages have roofs supported by huge beams from 400 or 500 years ago. The village derives its name from Sir William de Messing, who it seems made possible the building of the church. This is a lovely stroll through tranquil woodland areas and along the Rampart, probably once part of the defensive structure of nearby Haynes Green, before returning through Layer Wood.

The Old Crown Inn

The pub is a lovely old timbered building and from time to time has been visited by the Bush family of the former president of the USA, whose great grandfather lived in the village. The pub is noted for serving good beers brewed in Essex by Ridleys, but is well worth a visit for the food alone. There is a selection of traditional pub dishes, also some of a more unusual nature in a comprehensive menu. The restaurant is closed on Sunday evenings. Like certain other pubs in rural Essex the Old Crown doubles as a sub-post office on Mondays and Thursdays. Telephone: 01621 815575.

The Walk

① Leaving the pub cross the road along The Street past Crispins restaurant. Reaching the church and Donkin Hall follow the road to the right and then to the left.

② Just after Keepers Cottage turn left off the road by a concrete public footpath sign and cross a stile into a narrow path between a fence and a hedge. Continue up the hill to enter the wood. Turn left along a marked path. When you reach the remains of an old stile on your left, turn right and follow a path between the ferns going south through Conyfield Wood. Towards the end of the wood turn left at a hut and exit the wood over a plank bridge. Cross a stile and turn right along the fence to a stile onto the road.

③ Turn left along the road for a few yards and left over a stile for the path running south-east with a hedge or wood on your

The path through Conyfield Wood

PLACES OF INTEREST NEARBY

Colchester, to the north-east is a fascinating town. It boasts the largest Norman castle keep in Europe and has an excellent museum attached to it. Telephone: 01206 282931.

Part of the Rampart.

left, to the road (B1022). Cross carefully half left to a concrete public footpath sign and enter the wood. The path runs eastward crossing a track and continues through the wood. At the end take the farm track left and uphill, soon reaching the Rampart. The path follows on top of the Rampart then crosses two stiles to a small open field. Cross this to a yellow waymark half right, then turn left with the hedge on your right uphill to a road.

④ Turn left past the first house on your right and turn right along the grass track. Soon at a fork on the track keep to the left (north-east) and follow the track through the wood very straight north-west to a concrete public footpath sign by the B1022.

⑤ Turn right along this busy road for 300 yards. When you reach a public footpath sign on your left, turn left off the road and follow a concrete track downhill. At the bottom turn left and later bear right over a stile onto another concrete track. Turn right and then left following west towards the approaching Messing church. When the track turns left go straight on and through a gap in the houses. The Old Crown Inn is a few yards on your left.

Great Stambridge
The Royal Oak

MAP: OS EXPLORER 176 (GR 899919)   **WALK 23**   **DISTANCE:** 2¼ MILES

DIRECTIONS TO START: GREAT STAMBRIDGE IS NORTH-EAST OF ROCHFORD, OFF THE B1013. **PARKING:** THE LANDLORD IS HAPPY FOR YOU TO PARK IN THE ROYAL OAK CAR PARK WHILE YOU DO THE WALK BUT PLEASE LET THEM KNOW YOU ARE LEAVING YOUR CAR.

Under 3 miles north of Southend as the crow flies, arriving in Great Stambridge takes you back in time to a small country village. From here you walk along good paths to attractive Hampton Barns Farm. For those who wish, you can extend the walk onto the sea wall at Bartonhall Creek and take a break to look for any estuary birds before the return walk. Then take a route over a horse paddock and along the estate road to Brick House Farm passing a poultry farm and trout fisheries on the way. Now follows a short road walk that leads onto cross field paths that have unexpectedly long views over Southend and Rochford. The final approach to the pub is by a fascinating route first between paddocks then along a quiet road with lovely bungalows.

The Royal Oak

This old building currently falls into two areas, the first a large bar, the second the restaurant and bar on the right-hand side of the building. This is the part I like best with a very high ceiling that looks like a converted barn. You will find comfortable chairs and wall sofas to sit on, with polished wooden tables. You can choose a light lunch, two courses from the menu board, or you may be drawn to the full blackboard menu with starters like stilton stuffed mushrooms. The main courses on the day I was there included veal with a three-mustard sauce, and seafood pancakes. The pudding I would have liked to try was toffee and pecan cheesecake but alas even with the light menu choice of melon followed by roast beef I was full fit to busting. For those more interested in the drinks you will find Courage Best Bitter and Speckled Hen on hand pump. Also available are 1664, Beamish Red Irish Ale, Fosters and Strongbow cider. Telephone: 01702 258259.

The Walk

① From the Royal Oak turn right and cross the road. Turn left into Ash Tree Court. A footpath sign confirms your route. Walk to the right of the wire fence. When this runs out follow the path under the BT lines all the way to Hampton Barns. When you come to the estate road turn left still under the BT lines. White concrete bollards mark the edge of the road through the lovely farm steading.

② Just before the road turns left you have to make a sharp right-hand turn back on

yourself, but some may wish to take the opportunity of first climbing half right onto the sea wall for a rest. Now look out for the concrete footpath sign pointing just south of west – you have to follow the direction it is pointing in. This route takes you over two horse bars into a field and over a further two horse bars into a meadow. You walk ahead along the back of the gardens on your right. When you come to a gate go through it, turn left to cross a cattle grid and walk the route the locals take along the estate road back to Brick House Farm. The correct line of the footpath is to your left through the horse

PLACES OF INTEREST NEARBY

Southend Airport, just south-west of Rochford, is the place to go to watch the arrivals and departures of planes both large and small.

The Old House at 17 South Street, Rochford, built in 1270, has been restored and now houses the offices of the District Council. It is open every Wednesday from 2 pm to 4.30 pm. Telephone: 01702 318144 to book on the 40 minute guided tour.

Paddocks at point 5 of the walk.

meadows back to the bend in the road, but this is rather difficult to follow.

③ On reaching the road turn left and walk past the Old Rectory, now a nursing home. Take the first footpath sign on your right. You will be walking along a wide green path with the hedge on your right.

④ At a direction post with yellow arrows at the end of the garden turn right. Walk with a hedge on your right. At the next direction post walk straight across the next field. The path is normally well trodden.

The next direction post confirms you go straight on again with the hedge on your right.

⑤ About half way along this field turn right at a large wooden pole. Walk straight ahead on a wide green lane with horse paddocks on either side of the path. Climb the stile on your left and immediately cross a three-plank bridge. Turn right and walk with a fence on the left. Turn left to come out on a drive. Turn right passing lovely bungalows and in a few minutes you will reach the road, footpath sign and pub.

Althorne
The Three Horseshoes

| MAP: OS EXPLORER 176 (GR 916988) | WALK 24 | DISTANCE: 3¼ MILES |

DIRECTIONS TO START: ALTHORNE IS ON THE B1010, NORTH-WEST OF BURNHAM ON CROUCH. **PARKING:** AT THE THREE HORSESHOES, BUT PLEASE ASK FIRST.

The village of Althorne is built on the ridge between the rivers Blackwater and Crouch. The Three Horseshoes faces the River Crouch and as you descend the hill towards Althorne Creek you get superb views over Easter Reach, Canewdon church and on towards Southend on Sea. Having crossed the railway line you walk along the wild banks of Althorne Creek to Bridgemarsh Marina. The simple route back to the pub just follows the track till it becomes a road at the station. Once your legs confirm you have climbed some 130 feet uphill you reach the B1010. You make a small detour to visit the peaceful grounds of Althorne church. What we can never understand is how a landmark that is visible for so many miles across Essex appears to be on the flat when you get there.

The Three Horseshoes

This friendly pub is part of the Grays and Sons group. The main bar has a welcoming brick fireplace and there is also a restaurant available when the place is extra busy. There is a large well equipped children's play area and beer garden. A wide choice of food awaits you – I can recommend the home-made individual steak and kidney pie, which came with a choice of fresh vegetables and new potatoes. The curry was equally nice on the day we visited, when you could choose from beef madras or chicken balti. The regular specials board included other favourites like chilli and lasagne, while the standard menu had butterfly chicken breast and salmon Shanti to tempt you. Vegetarians are well catered for with no less than six menu choices. You may be less hungry and just want a sandwich, ploughman's or a jacket potato; there is a wide selection of fillings to choose from. Greene King's IPA and Tetleys are on handpump as is Strongbow cider. Telephone: 01621 740307.

The Walk

① From the pub turn right on the main road. After a few yards you come to Austral Cottages. Cross the road and turn left at footpath sign number 7. This gravel path takes you downhill. Just before you reach the private road sign, the path leaves the track right on a field path to the right of a hedge. There is a concrete slab on the ground at this point, perhaps the remains of the base of a garage. You have to walk across this to join the onward path.

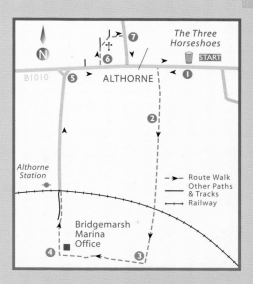

② As you descend you get excellent views of the creek ahead. As you descend further the track becomes a shady tunnel. It later becomes a field edge path but you still continue with the hedge on your left. At the railway gate check for any oncoming trains before you cross to the gate on the lower side of the track.

③ On joining the sea wall turn right with the creek on your left. When you come to Bridgemarsh Marina continue straight on to the right of the metal barrier to cross a stile.

④ Turn right up a gravel road. Ignore gravel roads to left and right of the main

PLACES OF INTEREST NEARBY
Mangapps Farm Railway Museum is at Southminster Road, Burnham on Crouch, a collection of railway relics including steam and diesel locos, wagons and carriages. Telephone: 01621 784898.

Upstream from Bridgemarsh marina.

track and continue uphill to the station. Enjoy the safety notices for lorries and tractors at the previous crossing point. Cross the railway line and continue uphill; it soon becomes a road.

⑤ At the T junction with the B1010 turn right and cross the road to the pavement on the left-hand side. You get super views back over the creek from here.

⑥ Turn left up a tarred drive to St Andrew's Vicarage; it is marked footpath 4 on the footpath sign. As the paths divide go through the church gates. Follow the route to the left of the church and then half right to exit from the far corner of the churchyard. A bridge helps you cross the stream and you soon join a gravel road. Turn right along Upper Chase and make your way out onto the road ahead.

⑦ Turn right and again cross to the footpath on the left of the road. At the T junction by Fords coaches turn left and make your way back to the pub.

Little Horkesley
The Beehive

MAP: OS EXPLORER 196 (GR 962321)   **WALK 25**   DISTANCE: 2¾ MILES

DIRECTIONS TO START: LITTLE HORKESLEY IS MIDWAY BETWEEN THE A134 AND THE B1508, NORTH-WEST OF COLCHESTER. **PARKING:** PARK AT THE BEEHIVE IN THE VILLAGE BUT PLEASE ASK FOR PERMISSION BEFORE SETTING OUT ON THE WALK.

This small and quite unassuming village inspires a great liking. Centuries ago there was a minor priory here belonging to the Cluniac order which was suppressed by Henry VIII and entirely destroyed. The medieval church was totally demolished in a bombing raid in 1940 and a replacement was completed in 1958. The immediate surroundings of Little Horkesley church, where this walk begins, are most delightful. A lovely plastered house stands beside the church and beyond the road the land drops down to give views towards Great Horkesley. In fact, this short stroll has exceptional views all round and especially over the Stour Valley to Nayland and Stoke by Nayland.

The Beehive

The Beehive has a character all of its own. At one time the pub sign was in part a real beehive! The pub building was also hit by a bomb in 1940 and rebuilt in 1954. A Greene King tenancy, the main beers are IPA and Abbott. For somewhere not so far from Colchester the atmosphere suggests the depths of the countryside. A varied selection of good food is available, and both the food and drinks are served in a very relaxed and friendly fashion. Telephone: 01206 271610.

The Walk

① From the pub turn right south down Vinesse Road. Just past the drive into the church and Little Horkesley Hall, turn right off the road at a concrete public footpath sign over a stile into a meadow. Walk down this past the church to trees at the bottom and reach two stiles into an arable field over a plank bridge. Go half right uphill to the right-hand end of the wood ahead.

Little Horkesley church.

Josslyns.

② Follow the field edge to your right. After 350 yards at a junction of paths where there are waymark arrows, the path continues with the hedge on your right and reaches Maltings Farm. From here the walk will be shepherded by the lovely sight of Stoke by Nayland church, sometimes with Nayland church below.

③ Turn right along the lane passing Jasmine Cottage. At a bend ignore the first footpath to climb up some steep steps by the second sign on the left. Walk down a good path by the hedge to waymarks near a telephone pole.

④ Turn right with the hedge on your right to follow the contour above the Stour Valley. At the top of an old road continue with the hedge now on your left for 250 yards. At the gap in the hedge take the path to the left.

⑤ At the bottom turn right by a stream through a gap in the facing hedge towards the wood (Creaks Grove).

⑥ Turn right uphill by the edge of the wood. At the top continue straight ahead on a grassy track towards Josslyns, a magnificent half timbered house. At Josslyns turn right up the road and soon reach the Beehive.

PLACES OF INTEREST NEARBY
After your walk around Little Horkesley, **Nayland** and **Stoke by Nayland** are both worth a visit as Suffolk border towns.

Layer Breton
The Hare and Hounds

MAP: OS EXPLORER 184 (GR 968200) **WALK 26** **DISTANCE:** 4 MILES WITH A 3½ MILE OPTION

DIRECTIONS TO START: LAYER BRETON IS SOUTH-WEST OF COLCHESTER, BETWEEN THE B1022 AND THE B1026. THE HARE AND HOUNDS PUB IS SITUATED ON THE EDGE OF BEAUTIFUL LAYER BRETON HEATH. **PARKING:** AVAILABLE IN THE HARE AND HOUNDS CAR PARK; LET SOMEONE AT THE PUB KNOW WHO OWNS THE CAR, PLEASE.

Layer Breton Heath makes a wonderful starting point for this walk, for after just a short stroll you will be enjoying great views over Abberton Reservoir, with the church and village of Abberton itself clearly visible at the top of the hill, looking over the water towards you. It is worth taking the time to include the walk to the Wildfowl Centre, on a trail that includes several of the hides where you can enjoy watching the wild life. Green lanes and field paths bring you back to Layer Breton's pretty heath.

The Hare and Hounds

This quaint pub retains a delightful series of small bars, while a huge brick fireplace with a welcoming fire in winter dominates the main bar. The choice of food at first may seem rather restricted but I can assure you – from simple beef or ham sandwiches, through their chicken and chips to exotic prawns in filo pastry or the more traditional ham, eggs and chips to steak done just the way you choose – you are in for a treat. You will find a range of Greene King IPA and Abbott plus Adnams Bitter. Also available are cider and a full range of both alcoholic and non alcoholic refreshments. There is a nice safe garden with a good supply of garden seating. Disabled facilities are available in this friendly pub which is open all day except Sunday when the hours are 12 noon to 3 pm and 7 pm to 10.30 pm. Bar snacks are available Sunday lunchtime but no food is served Sunday evening. Telephone: 01206 330459.

The Walk

① From the pub turn left and walk east along the road for about ¹/₃ mile. At the corner by the footpath sign take the farm track ahead over open fields.

② As the track turns right go half left over the field ahead to its far edge. At the hedge ahead go through the gap and walk to the right-hand side of the hedge, going south-east and east down to the B1026 Wigborough Road and footpath sign. Turn right and take care as the cars come rather fast along here. Those choosing the shorter walk will continue down the road to Point 5 below.

③ After ¹/₃ mile those doing the longer walk turn left into the entrance of the Wildfowl Centre. Follow the signs to the visitor centre and book in for your visit. Drinks and light refreshments are available from the cool cabinet. A small donation is expected to assist in the work of the trust. Follow the trail towards Wainwright Hide. Walk on the wooden walk boards and then turn right when you reach the sign to go round the peninsular (the sign comes up with its back towards you). You may have built in time to stop and watch the birds as you pass Roy King Hide or the Tony Soper Hide. Your route takes you as close to the reservoir as visitors are allowed.

④ As you approach the B1026 turn right through a gate and right again to keep on the path inside the reserve. When you come level with some old trees and a metal gate on your right, you will find a walkway left out onto the B1026, opposite a footpath sign and a route going north-west. Those taking the short cut will have walked on, on the road, to this point.

Young birdwatchers from the Wildfowl Centre.

⑤ Both parties now walk the waymarked road to Rows Farm. At the farm buildings turn right onto a farm track heading north, this very soon becomes a hedged green lane. When the hedge runs out on your right (this is about ¹/₃ mile after the farm) turn left through the gap indicated by the yellow arrow.

⑥ As you pop through the hole in the hedge you will find your route west along a well trodden path to the left of a hedge. At the end of the field turn right and cross a two-plank bridge. The yellow arrows direct you across the next field to the left of a pond. You are walking near the area where

PLACES OF INTEREST NEARBY

Colchester Zoo, Maldon Road, Stanway is just 2½ miles north of the pub. Telephone: 01206 331292.

Nevards Farm once stood. Turn right on reaching the track and walk north-west to the edge of Layer Breton Heath.

⑦ Just before you reach the road, turn left and take another turn half right to walk west across the heath parallel to the road back to the pub for your well earned choice of refreshments.

Bradwell Waterside
The Green Man Inn

MAP: OS EXPLORER 176 (GR 995078) | **WALK 27** | **DISTANCE:** 2¼ MILES

DIRECTIONS TO START: BRADWELL WATERSIDE IS AT THE END OF THE B1021 ON THE DENGIE PENINSULA. **PARKING:** BY PERMISSION OF THE LANDLORD IN THE PRIVATE GREEN MAN CAR PARK. THIS ESPECIALLY APPLIES IN THE BUSY SUMMER WEEKEND SESSIONS. IF IT IS JUST TOO BUSY YOU SHOULD FIND A SPACE ON THE ROAD NEAR THE WAR MEMORIAL, SEE (5) ON THE MAP, AND START THE WALK FROM THERE.

Bradwell Waterside is an interesting mixture of an old village and a very modern waterside sports resort. The stroll starts off near the creekside in the centre of the village and soon joins the sea wall with wide views over the creek and the river beyond. To your right are the towering Bradwell Power Station buildings and in fact the route passes just one field from their outer fences. Two pill boxes are a reminder of more dangerous times and the cross-field paths lead to the edge of RAF Bradwell. An interesting twitten leading to two cross-field paths and a further twitten make a nice end to this village walk.

The Green Man Inn

A very large fireplace with log fires gives a warming welcome on winter days. In view of its position it is not surprising to find so many seafaring items on the walls and shelves. There is a separate restaurant for those wishing to return for an evening meal. You will find an excellent selection of Nethergate beers including IPA, Bitter, and their seasonal brews. Bass is also available on hand pump. Alongside the full range of lagers, ciders and spirits is a choice of wines and several brands of champagne. There is a full range of snacks, sandwiches, ploughman's and jacket potatoes. The large blackboard menu is changed every three months but the favourites like steak and ale pie, and fish and chips are normally available. I would recommend the salmon and halibut Wellington if you want a light meal. The pub also has accommodation for those wishing to stay overnight. Telephone: 01621 776226.

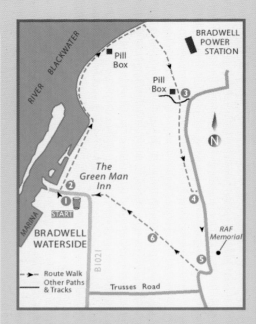

The Walk

① From the pub car park turn left down the road and go as far as the red and white barrier gate to get your first view of Bradwell Creek and to see the boating. Now retrace your steps about 10 paces till you are level with the Bradwell Outdoor Education Centre. Climb up the slope on your right, onto the sea wall.

② There is a seat here if you want to rest a while and just admire the views. Your onward route takes you north-east along the sea wall. You pass a caravan site on your right and continue right round the sea wall till you come to a pill box near where the

creek joins the River Blackwater. About 250 paces further on you come to a wooden sign on the sea wall leading right towards the line of wooden fencing and a second pill box on a field edge. This is your route. You are just one field back from Bradwell Power Station.

③ After you pass the second pill box you walk slightly uphill to a green metal gate

PLACES OF INTEREST NEARBY

For **Bradwell Power Station** and visitor centre just follow the brown visitor signs out to the centre or make a detour further along the sea wall from (2) and take the permissive path right into the car park and to the centre. Closed in the winter months.

St Peter's on the Wall, Bradwell on Sea is a 7th century Saxon chapel. Go through the village and out to the coast.

Bradwell Creek.

and enter a gravel road. Continue in the same direction up the road and as it bends left go straight on into a green hedged path. A yellow arrow helps you to find this turn. This well walked path takes you between two fields and about 20 feet from a road on your left. Continue on this path till you reach the end of the undergrowth. A yellow arrow confirms two paths now divide. You need to turn sharp left to a footpath sign well hidden in an apple tree at the road side.

④ Turn right and walk beside the road to the wire fence. If you cross the road here you will soon find another track, which enables you to continue ahead with the road on your right. You soon reach the memorial to the men of RAF Bradwell Bay who served from 1942 to 1945.

⑤ Having stopped to pay your respects,

rejoin the road turning right and left to its junction with Trusses Road. On your right at this bend you will find a footpath sign and a gravel track. Take this along the backs of gardens. The path soon has a wire fence on your right and the gardens continue on your left. When these run out your route is straight on over a cross-field path to the five tall trees you can see straight ahead.

⑥ Under the trees you will find three wooden posts with yellow arrows and a gap in the fence. Go through this and walk along the new fence line past one tree and at the second, by a yellow arrow, you have to cross a second field. Turn right on a well cut path to waymark and metal poles that form a kissing gate exit. This brings you into a path between houses and out onto the road near the centre of the village. Continue ahead down this road to the pub.

Langham
The Shepherd and Dog

MAP: OS EXPLORER 196 (GR 019318)   **WALK 28**   **DISTANCE:** 3¾ MILES

DIRECTIONS TO START: TURN OFF THE A12 NORTH OF COLCHESTER WHEN MARKED LANGHAM, TO GO ALONG PARK LANE. TURN RIGHT AT THE T JUNCTION AND TAKE THE VILLAGE ROAD PAST THE POST OFFICE TO THE SHEPHERD AND DOG AT BLACKSMITHS CORNER. **PARKING:** PARK AT THE PUB BUT PLEASE ASK PERMISSION TO LEAVE YOUR CAR BEFORE GOING ON THE STROLL.

The area between here and the Stour Valley on the Suffolk border contains some of the most beautiful walking country in Essex. Langham is most famous for its association with John Constable. The church stands high on a hill above the Stour Valley (Dedham Vale) and the tower was started in the 13th century to be completed in Tudor times. Constable was a lifelong friend of John Fisher the curate, and would frequently climb by ladder to the top of the tower to sit and work on the view. The church appears in Constable's painting of Glebe Farm (passed on the walk).

The Shepherd and Dog

The pub is unusual these days – a successful business enterprise in the middle of the countryside. At lunch time it is very orientated to food. The selection of well cooked dishes here includes almost everything you have thought of and they are quite willing to serve a bowl of chips with sandwiches. The menu includes fish and vegetarian dishes, starters, main courses and desserts. The main problem you will have is limiting your choice to a few from which to make a selection. Coffee is readily available when you have finished and just want t o complete the meal. There are usually four or five real ales on the pump such as Greene King IPA. Adnams and Nethergate to slake a dry walker's thirst. The busy time is 12.30 pm to 1.30 pm so it may be more relaxing to time your visit outside these hours. At any rate it is a fine pub and well run at all times. Telephone: 01206 272711.

The Walk

① Walk north opposite the pub up Guchard Hill.

② After 350 yards turn right at a concrete public footpath post along a fenced path. Bear slightly right at a yellow arrow waymark and cross two stiles, passing a large collection of free range hens. Now you must negotiate an electric fence by unhooking a handle to get through.

③ Replace the handle and turn sharp left, aiming to the right of the pond ahead. Behind the pond at the corner of the field go through the right-hand gate marked with a yellow arrow to walk through woodland with the fence on your left. Come out to a sloping grass lawn with ponds at the bottom and continue to an arrow at a stile. After another stile turn half right to cross a bridge over a stream to a stile.

④ Turn left, crossing Black Brook, and right at the bridleway sign. Go straight on past the house on the left and stay on this way, passing Glebe Farm and Glebe House and all the time seeing Langham church in the distance. When you reach a road, turn

PLACES OF INTEREST NEARBY

The **Sir Alfred Munnings Art Museum** at Castle House, Dedham is set in the home, studios and grounds where Sir Alfred lived and painted for 40 years. Admission charge. Open Sunday, Wednesday and Bank Holiday Mondays, May to September, 2 pm to 5 pm. Telephone: 01206 322127.

Dedham Art and Craft Centre is in the High Street, open 10 am to 5 pm. Small admission charge. Telephone: 01206 322666.

A picturesque cottage at the start of the walk.

right and then left down the drive to the church and also Langham Hall.

⑤ Turn right at the corner and left at the church. Here the lane is marked public footpath only. This church is depicted in some of Constable's famous paintings of Dedham Vale. Walk downhill on the track passing a wood on your left. Here you will have a wonderful view of the Stour Valley.

⑥ At a crossing hedge turn sharply to the left with a yellow arrow and walk alongside the hedge to a stile. Cross the field in the same direction to another stile and bridge onto a farm road. Turn left along this road to reach a public road. Cross over the road and follow the Essex Way sign, soon crossing an open field to another road. Leave the Essex Way here and turn left to reach the major road near a corner.

⑦ Turn left for a few yards and right at a footpath sign along the left-hand side of a hedge to a little wood. Turn right and walk round the outside of the wood. On reaching Hill Farm follow the arrows first right and then left of the perimeter wall.

⑧ Walk past the farmhouse and turn left immediately to cross a stile, going south into a small stretch of woodland. The path goes downhill and then up past the stream (yes, it's the Black Brook again!). Continue south aiming ahead for a house. At the fence surrounding this house turn left and right with the fence, and turn right off the field at the front of the garage onto the drive which leads to a road. Now turn left for a few yards back to the Shepherd and Dog.

Lawford
The King's Arms

MAP: OS EXPLORER 184 (GR 085312) **WALK 29** **DISTANCE:** 2½ MILES

DIRECTIONS TO START: LAWFORD IS ABOUT 2 MILES FROM ARDLEIGH ON THE A137. THE KING'S ARMS IS ON THE MAIN ROAD AS YOU ENTER THE VILLAGE. **PARKING:** IN THE PUB CAR PARK BUT ENSURE THE LANDLORD KNOWS YOU ARE THERE. ALSO WHEN THE CHURCH IS NOT IN USE PARKING IS POSSIBLE AT (5).

Views over the beautiful Stour Valley accompany the first part of this short stroll out from Lawford. The Essex Way brings your first glimpses over Lawford Park. You soon walk up the drive towards Lawford Hall, a timbered building erected in the 16th century and into the churchyard. In the church you will find a memorial to Edward Waldegrave, who died when the Hall was new. There is also a tablet to Dean Merivale, rector for over 20 years but more famous because he rowed in the first university boat race. Your views are over Manningtree as you descend to Wignall Brook and the return walk along the banks of this small brook is very rural.

The King's Arms

This pub is so easy to find just on the outskirts of Manningtree. The pretty garden is set on a hill with a fenced duck pond as its centrepiece. The pub is much older than you may at first think with parts said to date from the 16th century. It is divided into two main areas, with the old public bar well supported by card and darts players. The other bar is a fine eating area. You will in fact discover the expected wooden beams and fine brick fireplaces. Behind the bar you will find Greene King IPA, Speckled Hen and Adnams on hand pump alongside Strongbow cider. Menu choices include a fine range of home-made pies including chicken and mushroom, and sausage and onion. On Sundays, of course, a roast dinner awaits you. For more information ring 01206 392758.

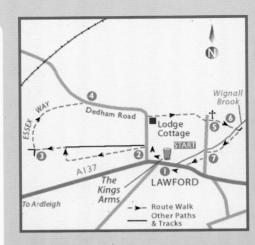

The Walk

① From the pub turn right to walk the 50 or so yards west along the A137. Turn right into Dedham Road and in ⅛ mile look for a double footpath sign on your left.

② The footpath route goes directly west, but when the crops are high you may wish to take the route the locals do. You would go up the side of the orchard to join the permissive path, turn right along the field end and join the true footpath just as the path turns left. The yellow arrows confirm your route is over the stile into the meadow, then you walk with the hedge on your left to cross another stile.

③ You have now joined the Essex Way and a blue arrow confirms you are in the right place. Turn right up this gravel drive. Where the track divides take the one on the right. Go through two metal gates on your way out to the road. What super views you get along this part of the walk.

④ On reaching the road turn right and walk with care round the right-hand bend. You are now looking for a lodge cottage on your left. The footpath sign is hidden to the left-hand side of the drive it guards. You are still on the Essex Way and your route ahead is up the old drive. Follow the Essex Way signs to the church.

⑤ Go through the church gate into the

PLACES OF INTEREST NEARBY

Mistley Place Park and Animal Rescue Centre in New Road, Mistley has 2½ acres of parkland with over 2,000 rescued animals. Telephone 01206 396483 for more details.

The **Essex Secret Bunker**, Shrublands Road, Mistley is a former nuclear war HQ set in a concrete bunker. Telephone: 01206 392271 for opening hours.

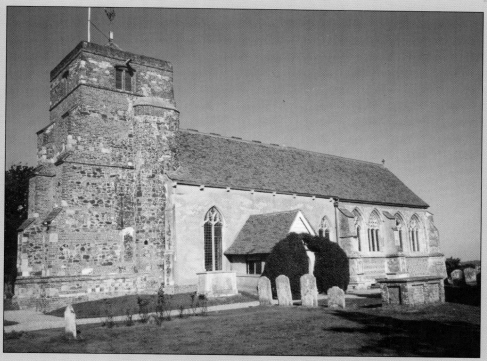

Lawford church.

churchyard and leave time to explore this beautiful red brick and flint building. When you are ready to leave go to the rear right-hand side of the church wall and you will find the stile that brings you out to rejoin the Essex Way.

⑥ Walk downhill on the routeway marked for you. Cross Wignall Brook and then turn right and cross a two-plank bridge. Your route ahead is just to the left of the brook on the edge of a large meadow.

⑦ On reaching the end of the field (sometimes damp for the last few yards), go through the kissing gate and out on to the road. Turn left and then right to cross a stile. Your route over this meadow is under the oak trees on a well walked track to the stile ahead. Cross this and make your way onto the road. Turn right and walk the few yards back to your car.

Little Oakley
Ye Olde Cherry Tree

MAP: OS EXPLORER 184 (GR 217291) **WALK 30** **DISTANCE:** 3 MILES

DIRECTIONS TO START: LITTLE OAKLEY IS ABOUT 1 MILE SOUTH OF THE A120(T) JUST WEST OF HARWICH. **PARKING:** IN YE OLDE CHERRY TREE'S CAR PARK OR ON THE ROAD BETWEEN THE PUB AND THE SCHOOL, MAKING SURE YOU DO NOT BLOCK ANYONE'S DRIVEWAY.

Leaving the village on the road north passing the school, you soon join a bridleway with super views of Ramsey windmill and church as you descend into the valley. A walk over ancient meadows follows and an uphill climb to the ridge. A stroll through the outskirts of the village takes you back to the footpath system and a cross field path up to the ridge. From here you can seen over Bramble and Pewit Islands to Hamford Water. A disused church is the main point of interest on the return walk to the pub and a welcome drink and bite to eat.

Ye Olde Cherry Tree

The long bar is dominated by a large stone fireplace, a brick and wooden bar, and wooden beams in the ceilings all combining to give a welcoming appearance in this pub that is in fact much older than it seems. It had a priest's hole on the first floor and some claim it is 15th century. Behind the bar of this freehouse you will find a selection of real ales including Bombardier, Adnams Broadside, Eagle and Happy Top. There is a regular menu and a blackboard specials menu; one choice I liked the sound of was Honey Chicken Kebab with peanut sauce. I also noted a number of fish dishes and curry. Sandwiches, ploughman's, salads, vegetarian meals and grills are available. I enjoyed a super Sunday roast and can recommend this. There is also a range of take-away foods. The pub displays a certificate confirming they were highly commended in the Homefire Real Fire Pub of the year award of 1999. Telephone: 01255 880333.

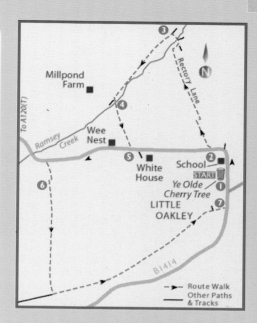

The Walk

① From the pub turn left and pass Cherry Tree Close and the infants' school. Ignore the footpath sign on your right and cross Oak Lodge. Ignore the next footpath sign and walk on to the bridleway sign.

② Turn right and walk on this wide track (named Rectory Lane on the map). You soon get excellent views over Ramsey to the church and the windmill. Follow the track as it turns right and left as it makes its way downhill. Turn right at a six-bar gate and soon reach a track. Go straight over this,

walking to the left of a brick pillar. Cross a wooden bridge over Ramsey Creek and a stile to enter a large meadow. Your route is to the far hedge.

③ Turn left and walk with the hedge on your right. Cross a stile bridge and stile (both cross members were missing the day we walked it out). When the hedge turns right spot Millpond Farm house on your right and turn left to cross the field to a gate and stile.

PLACES OF INTEREST NEARBY
Harwich is full of interesting places to see. These include the Redoubt, a fort built in 1808–1810; the Ha'penny Visitor Centre at the Quay; the Lifeboat Museum in Timerfields off Wellington Road; the Harwich Maritime Museum in Harbour Crescent; and the Electric Light Cinema. For details on all of these telephone the Tourist Information Centre: 01255 503429.

Ramsey seen across the fields.

④ Cross the river on a wide concrete bridge. As you climb this green field, take a line just right of the hedge and come to a stile. You will probably wish to stop and admire the views on the way up. Cross the stile which is just to the right of the gate. Walk down the drive to the road and footpath sign.

⑤ Turn right and walk past a row of houses with names like Wee Nest. The road drops down a hill as it leaves the ridge. On your left you will find a footpath sign and a cross-field path. Walk south-east to the stile bridge and two steps which take you into the next field.

⑥ Now walk straight on up the hill with the ditch on your left to a large oak tree. You are just at the rear of Great Oakley Hall. Turn left on a green track with good views over to the coast. Walk past St Mary's old church, now a private house. It is claimed there was once a tunnel from here to the pub, probably in the days when priests had to hide in a hurry. Walk straight on with a footpath sign on your left. Continue ahead at the next yellow arrow and this will bring you onto a cross-field path that leads out to the road.

⑦ At the road and footpath sign turn left for the short walk back to your car.